REAL PROPERTY

LawPrep™

LawPrep™
2698 White Road
Irvine, California 92714
800-359-7737

"This publication is designed to provide accurate and authoritative information in regard to the subject matter covered. It is sold with the understanding that the publisher is not engaged in rendering legal, accounting, or other professional services. If legal advice or other expert assistance is required, the services of a competent professional person should be sought."

From the declaration of Principles jointly adopted by a Committee of the American Bar Association and a Committee of Publishers and Associations.

Printed in the United States of America

CONTENTS

SUMMARY

The study of real property focuses on rights, duties, and interests pertaining to land. Much of the real-property law you will study in law school is derived from the English common-law system. Many of the rules pertaining to areas such as future interests may appear archaic but are essential in understanding this field of law for law school and bar examination purposes.

This book will give you an overview of the basic principles of real property as taught in law school. It will emphasize land rights as well as water and airspace rights.

In studying real property, it is important to determine issues, such as:

1. How land is held, issues pertaining to title and ownership,
2. Are there easments or covenants which affect the land?
3. Are there problems which suggest an interference with one's legal right to own and posses the land?

These are a few of the questions which are useful in approaching any real property question.

INTRODUCTION

This book will explain the rules of law in the difficult area of future interests with simple explanations and tricks for learning the rules of law. You will learn how property is possessed; how interests in land are created, transferred, and terminated; the varieties of easements and covenants; how property records are maintained; and how title is conveyed. The topics have been arranged to present the material in an organized and systematic method to help you understand the subject matter. Although the organization of the topics in this book may differ from standard first-year casebooks, it is, nevertheless, important that each student, when reading an assignment in law school, be aware of the chapter headings and try to place the subject matter within the context of this book.

. This book also contains basic discussions and ways to approach the various subjects regarding real property. It is not complete and may exceed or fail to cover certain areas in a standard first-year casebook. It is

LawPrep's intention to familiarize you with general principles of real-property law and to acquaint you with certain cases of particular importance in any first-year real property class.

REAL PROPERTY IN GENERAL

The term ***real property*** is used to describe the legal rights a person can have in real estate. There are three main areas of real property: (i) ownership interests, (ii) conveyance, and (iii) acquisition.

Ownership in land includes topics such as landlord-tenant and concurrent ownership, adverse possession, present and future interests, easements, and covenants running with the land.

Conveyancing refers to the transfer of land. The two main aspects of transfer are the execution and delivery of the deed. A discussion of conveyances would not be complete without a description of title assurance, recordation of the transfer of land, and other property documentation.

Acquisition of real property relates to how one comes into its possession. A person can acquire property through adverse possession, finding, inheritance, or through rights established by law.

THINKING ABOUT REAL PROPERTY

In thinking about the subject matter of real property, it is important to consider a few basic questions. This analysis will help you understand where you are in the area of real property and will help you identify issues and material facts in your real-property casebook. Remember, many cases deal with isolated issues and may assume certain elements have been satisfied. For example, if a case involves whether there has been a proper delivery of a deed, the focus may not be on whether title to the property was marketable. For purposes of writing law-school essay examinations, it is always important to consider all of the elements and to apply the facts to determine if an element is present, should be discussed, or should be dismissed as a non-material issue.

Consider the following questions when addressing a real property question:

1. Who is in possession?
2. How did he or she come into possession?
3. Has the property been or will the property be transferred?
4. Was the property properly transferred?
5. Are there any restrictions on the transfer?

If you are able to answer these questions, then you will have a good basis on which to answer an examination question. Although it is important to recognize whether these elements are present in any given question, the main issue of an examination question may focus on only, or a few of, these questions.

THEORIES OF REAL PROPERTY

Real property can be approached from three methods. One method allows you to examine how real property is held or possessed. A second method focuses on how real property is conveyed. A third method concerns rights relating to land. It is important to understand the difference between real property and personal property. Real property refers to any property which is attached to the land, such as fences, walls, trees, and buildings. Personal property refers to all other things that are not real property.

Much of American real-property law is based on early English common law. Many of the terms and concepts date back to feudal times, yet are still relevant today.

POSSESSORY INTERESTS IN LAND

In General

The concept of real property is meaningful only if it is associated with the person or legal entity that owns or possesses it. Terms such as "ownership," "title," and "possession" are often used to describe this relationship.

Ownership refers to someone who owns all the rights or interests associated with a piece of land. The term *title* is often used synonymously with ownership, but it also refers to the way in which a piece of property was acquired and is currently owned.

What does it mean to possess a piece of land, as compared to owning it? The concept of *possession* relates not only to immediate physical custody of real property but also to the power to obtain physical control by legal means. *Possession* is "that condition of facts under which one can exercise his power over a corporeal thing at his pleasure to the exclusion of all other persons." (*Black's Law Dictionary, 5th Edition.*)

Ways to Possess or Hold Real Property

There are a number of ways a person or entity can hold land, either as a means of ownership or possession:

1. Adverse possession;
2. Estates in land;
3. Concurrent ownership;
4. Landlord-tenant relationship;
5. Easements; and
6. Covenants running with the land.

Adverse Possession

Adverse possession is one way a person can hold an interest in land. It is "a method of acquisition of title to real property by possession for a statutory period under certain conditions." (*Black's Law Dictionary, 5th Edition.*) The theory of adverse possession states that if a person who does not own land possesses it for a period of time as specified in a state statute of limitations, then he or she may acquire title to the land if certain other requirements are satisfied. Although some states vary, most states allow a person to take possession if they have "possessed" the land for a period ranging from five to twenty-one years.

There are four requirements to prove adverse possession. They are:

1. Actual entry and possession of the land;
2. Open and notorious possession;
3. Continuous possession; and
4. Adverse possession

Actual Entry and Possession

A person must make an actual entry onto the land and take possession of the land. This does not mean that the person has to be constantly present, but it requires that there be some activity on the land. Any ordinary activity will constitute actual possession, but asserting a mere claim to the property will not.

For example, John has farmed the land of his adjacent neighbor Cranor for over 25 years, believing it to be his own. Even though he has not lived on it, the fact that he has farmed and harvested the land will probably be enough to satisfy the actual entry and possession of the land requirement.

Open and Notorious Possession

The second element of adverse possession is that the possession must be open and notorious. What does open and notorious mean? The possessor must act in a sufficiently public way to put the public on notice that he or she is on the land and in possession of the property. He or she is not required to record the property. The possessor is not required to notify the owner of the possessor's possession of the land. Therefore, it is up to the owner to make periodic inspections of his or her property so as to remain informed regarding possession of the land.

Continuous Possession

The third element of adverse possession requires that the possession be continuous. Continuous does not mean the possession must be constant. An activity will be considered constant if it is limited, but on a regular basis. Also, behavior which is considered continuous for an owner will be deemed continuous for an adverse possessor.

An adverse possession must be uninterrupted. Therefore, there can be no other person who is in possession of the property against the adverse possessor during the statutory period. If the possession is interrupted by a third person or the owner, the statute will stop running if the conflicting possession is made against the adverse possessor. An adverse possessor can add the possession of previous owners to his time if they were in privity with him. *Privity* is the "mutual or successive relationship to the same rights of property." (*Black's Law Dictionary, 5th Edition.*) Two or more time periods may be linked together under a principle known as tacking.

For example, if Gina purchased property from her predecessor, Eric, and took possession, she could tack Eric's time to her own. Privity of possession and not title is the key consideration.

Adverse Possession

The final element of adverse possession is that the possession be adverse. In other words, the possession may not result from the owner's permission or consent. Generally, an objective standard is applied to the term adverse. It does not refer to the subjective mental states of the parties. The possession must warn the owner of an actionable claim and entitle him or her to begin ejectment procedures.

HELPFUL HINT #1

DEFINITIONS

1. **REAL PROPERTY:** The legal rights a person can have in real property.
2. **CONVEYANCE**: The transfer of land.
3. **ACQUISITION**: The way one comes into possession.
4. **OWNERSHIP**: Someone who owns all the rights or interests in the real property.
5. **ADVERSE POSSESSION:** A method by which a non-owner of real property may acquire ownership of real property.

ESTATES IN LAND

The second way in which one may own or possess land is through an *estate in land*. *Estates in land* evolved during the feudal ages in England. There are *present estates* and *future estates*. *A present estate* is "an estate in immediate possession..." (*Black's Law Dictionary, 5th Edition.*) *A future estate* "...is an estate which is not now vested in the grantee, but is to commence in possession at some future time..." (Black's Law Dictionary, 5th Edition).

Present Estates

Present estates in land can also be classified as either *freehold estates or leasehold estates*. *A freehold estate* "...is a right of title to land." (Black's Law Dictionary, 5th Edition). A *leasehold estate* is "an estate in realty held under a lease." (*Black's Law Dictionary, 5th Edition.*)

All *present estates* in land, whether *freehold* or *leasehold*, can be categorized based on their duration, that is, when and how they end.

There are three main types of freehold estates:

1. Fee simple;
2. Fee tail; and
3. Life estate.

Fee Simple

The *fee simple* "...is an estate limited absolutely to a man and his heirs and assigns forever without limitation or condition." (*Black's Law Dictionary, 5th Edition.*) It is an absolute grant by the grantor to the grantee with no limitations as to its duration. Since it is inheritable by heirs of the owner, it has the potential of enduring forever. Language that is typically used to convey a fee-simple estate is, "O to A and his heirs," "O to A in fee simple absolute," "O to A," or "O to A in fee simple."

Fee Tail

The *fee tail* is the next most enduring common-law estate. A *fee tail* is "a freehold estate in which there is a fixed line of inheritable succession limited to the issue of the body of the grantee or devisee, and in which the regular and general succession of heirs at law is cut off." (*Black's Law Dictionary, 5th Edition.*) In other words, the estate is inheritable by issue of the then current owner, but not by collateral heirs. Therefore, children will take but not parents, cousins, aunts, etc. The majority of jurisdictions have abolished or modified the *fee tail*. In some courts, attempting to create a *fee tail* is treated as creating a *fee simple*. Language that is typically used to convey a fee tail is, "O to A and the heirs of his body."

Life Estate

The third type of *freehold estate* is a *life estate*. A *life estate* is "an estate whose duration is limited to the life of the party holding it, or some other person." (*Black's Law Dictionary, 5th Edition.*) This estate cannot be inherited, and therefore endures only as long as the holder of the estate lives. Typical language used for conveyance is "O to A for life," "O to A until A dies," or "O to A during his lifetime."

Leasehold Estates

The *leasehold estates*, also known as *nonfreehold estates*, all have theoretically ascertainable termination dates. They are classified by the way they are terminated. The three main *leasehold estates* are: (I) *tenancy for a term;* (II) *periodic tenancy;* and (III) *tenancy at will.* These will be covered under the *Landlord-Tenant* section. An estate which is subject to termination upon a naturally occurring event, such as death or the end of the term as described above, is known as an *absolute estate*. An estate may also be conditioned to terminate upon the happening of some event other than death or completion of the term. An estate which is limited in this way is referred to as a *defeasible estate*.

An estate which ends automatically and reverts automatically to the grantor if some named event occurs is called a *determinable estate*. Language which creates a *determinable estate is* "as long as..." or "until..."

Sometimes a *determinable estate* is referred to as an *estate subject to an executory limitation*. This will occur if the estate is made subject to automatic termination and the estate passes to a third party rather than reverting back to the grantor. For example, "To George and his heirs, so long as liquor is never sold upon the property, and if liquor is sold then to Louise and her heirs." If the grantee, George has a fee simple determinable, then the grantor will always have a possibility of reverter.

An estate can be drafted subject to *elective* rather than *automatic termination*. Such an estate is referred to as one *subject to a condition subsequent*. *A condition subsequent* is one in which, if it occurs, brings about the destruction of an existing interest. The following language creates a *condition subsequent:* "provided that ...", "but if...", or "on condition that..."

Consider the following example: "To Jan for life, but if I return from my trip unharmed, I may take back my estate." Jan has created a *life estate subject to a condition subsequent.* If the grantee has a fee simple subject to a condition subsequent, then the grantor will always have a right of re-entry.

Future Estates

A *future estate* does not allow a person holding land to take possession now but provides that he or she can do so in the future. There are five main types of future interests. They are classified according to whether they are held by the grantor or by a third person.

The five main types of future interests are:

1. Possibility of reverter;
2. Power of termination;
3. Executory interest;
4. Remainder; and
5. Reversion.

Possibility of Reverter

The *possibility of reverter* is an interest which is retained by a grantor. When the grantor grants a fee simple determinable, a possibility of reverter will vest automatically in the grantor. For example, Steven, holding in fee simple absolute, granted Greenacre, "To Michael and his heirs for so long as liquor is not sold on the premises..." Steven has a *fee simple determinable* and Michael has a *possibility of reverter*.

Power of Termination

The *power of termination* or *right of re-entry*, the second type of future interest, is an interest which is retained by the grantor following the conveyance of a fee simple subject to a condition subsequent. The estate is given on a *condition subsequent*. If the *condition subsequent* occurs, the grantor may elect to bring about a forfeiture of the estate and a transfer of title. The grantor has the option to terminate the estate for the violation of the condition and re-enter the premises. This requires action on the part of the grantor and is different from a *possibility of reverter* which will occur automatically if the event specified in the *fee simple determinable* occurs.

For example, Ralph holds a fee simple absolute and grants Greenacre "To Amy and her heirs, but if any of them ever sells liquor on the premises, then I or my heirs may re-enter and terminate their estate." In this scenario, Ralph has a *power of termination* or *right of re-entry*.

Both the *possibility of reverter* and the *power of termination* cut short prior estates. Both are interests created only in a grantor, but the *possibility of reverter* is fully transferrable to third persons thereafter; the *power of termination* is only transferrable in some jurisdictions.

Executory Interest

The third type of future interest is an *executory interest*. An *executory interest* is an interest created in a third person when the grantor has created a defeasible estate in the grantee. There are two types of *executory interests: shifting executory interests* and *springing executory interests.*

In a *shifting executory interest*, the interest "shifts" from one person to another. The shifting will cut short the first estate. For example, Iggy conveys Blackacre "to Joshua, but if Alex returns from the war alive, then to Alex." The estate will shift to Alex if he returns from the war alive. Alex's interest is executory because it is not vested; it is a future interest.

In a *springing executory interest*, the interest "springs" up out of the grantor's estate some time in the future. Consider the following example. Tammy conveys Blackacre "to Rex, and if Rex should die before Peter then to John." John has a future executory interest which will spring into existence if Rex should die before Peter.

Remainder

A *remainder* is the fourth type of *future interest*. It is an interest created in a third person which is capable of becoming a present possessory interest at the expiration of the prior estate. A *remainder* never cuts short or divests the prior estate. There are two types of *remainders: vested remainders* and *contingent remainders*.

A *vested remainder* is given to an ascertained person and is not subject to a condition precedent. For example, a grantor could create a *vested remainder* in "my sister Anita," or "my children" (if the grantor already has children).

A *contingent remainder* is a *remainder* which is not created in an ascertained person. For example, "To Estelle for life and then to Harry's widow and her heirs." In this scenario, Harry's widow is unascertained. His widow may or may not be his present wife, depending upon whether she remains married to him and survives his death. Estelle has a *life estate* and Harry's widow has a *contingent remainder in fee simple*.

There are three categories of *vested contingent remainders*:

1. Indefeasibly vested contingent remainder;
2. Vested remainder subject to open; and
3. Vested remainder subject to complete defeasance.

A *vested contingent remainder* that is *indefeasibly vested* is one which meets two tests. First, the holder of the remainder is certain to acquire a possessory estate. Second, upon receiving the estate, he or she is entitled to retain it permanently. Consider the following example: Greg conveys Whiteacre "to Alice for life, then to B and his heirs." B has an *indefeasible vested remainder*. B is certain to acquire the estate when Alice dies, and once he has acquired it, B is entitled to keep it permanently.

The second type of *vested contingent remainder* is called a *vested remainder subject to open*. It is the same as the *vested contingent remainder* with one exception. The "holder" of the remainder is usually a class of persons which may expand. For example, George conveys Greenacre "to Olivia for life, remainder to Olivia's children." Olivia may have had two children at the time this conveyance was written, but she may have more before her death.

The third type of *vested contingent remainder* is called a *vested remainder subject to complete defeasance*. This *vested remainder* is subject to being divested by the occurrence of a condition subsequent or may be divested if there is an inherent limitation on the remainder. For example, Gilda conveys Blackacre "to Ari for life, then to Craig, but if Craig does not survive Ari, then to Craig's oldest surviving son." In this situation, Craig has a remainder. However, if Craig does not survive Ari, then Craig will be divested of the remainder.

Reversion

A *reversion* is the fifth type of *future interest*. A *reversion* is "any future interest left in a transferor or his successor." (*Black's Law Dictionary, 5th Edition.*) Any time an estate which is granted to another does not equal the size of the estate held by the grantor, the grantor retains a reversion. *A reversion is like a remainder in that it vests upon the natural termination of the prior interest.*

For example, Oliver, holding an estate in *fee simple absolute*, grants Greenacre "to Andrea for life and then to Bradley for life." Since the two life estates do not add up to a fee simple absolute, Oliver retains a *reversion in fee simple* following Andrea's life estate and Bob's remainder.

Concurrent Ownership

Concurrent ownership is a third way to hold or possess land. *Concurrent ownership* occurs when two or more persons share the ownership of some estate in land. There are four types of *concurrent ownership*:

1. Joint tenancy;
2. Tenancy in common;
3. Tenancy by the entirety; and
4. Community property.

Joint Tenancy

Joint tenancy is the "type of ownership of real or personal property by two or more persons in which each owns an undivided interest in the whole and attached to which is the right of survivorship." (*Black's Law Dictionary, 5th Edition.*) The distinguishing characteristic of *joint tenancy* is the *right of survivorship*. Since each *joint tenant* is regarded as owning the entire estate, upon the death of one, the other's complete interest vests in the other. The survivor is not treated as one who inherits from the decedent but who has rights to full and complete possession. For example, Suzy and Carl were *joint tenants*. When Suzy died, she left a will in favor of Jimmy. Carl will prevail over Jimmy under the doctrine of survivorship and now owns the entire estate.

How is a *joint tenancy* created? At common law, four requirements, or unities, were necessary:

1. Unity of time;
2. Unity of title;
3. Unity of interest; and
4. Unity of possession.

Under the *unity of time*, all joint tenants must take their interests at the same time. Therefore, if Gary conveyed one-half of Whiteacre to Jacob last month and the other one-half interest to Larry last week, Jacob and Larry are not *joint tenants* because they have not taken their respective interests at the same time.

A *unity of title* requires that all parties take by the same instrument to qualify as *joint tenants*, whether it is by deed or will. This requirement is carefully scrutinized by the courts. For example, courts will not allow a spouse to convey property to himself and his wife as joint tenants because at common law no one could convey property to himself. Some statutes today give this type of conveyance the effect of a *joint tenancy*.

Under *unity of interest*, all of the *joint tenants* must hold equal interests, both as to size and duration. Any difference between their interests defeats the creation of the *joint tenancy*. After the tenancy is created, however, the tenants can agree that only one of them is to have actual possession of the property. For example, "Two-thirds to Curly and one-third to Jane as joint tenants." There is no *joint tenancy* despite what the grant says because the parties to do not have equal interests.

Unity of possession is the fourth *unity* which must be present in a *joint tenancy*. This *unity* states that each *tenant* has the right to possess the entire property. After the tenancy is created, the tenants can agree that only one of them is to have actual possession of the property.

Tenancy in Common

Tenancy in common is the second type of *concurrent ownership*. It is "a form of ownership whereby each tenant (i.e., owner) holds an undivided interest in property." (*Black's Law Dictionary, 5th Edition.*) A *tenancy in common* is applied in situations where no other form of *concurrent ownership* has been explicitly designated, or when the grant specifies that ownership shall be held in *tenancy in common*. Therefore, if Paul grants "to Amelia and Rob" and says nothing more, the conveyance will be considered a *tenancy in common*. Also, "To Amelia and Rob as tenants in common" will create a *tenancy in common estate*.

The principle difference between the *tenancy in common* and *the joint tenancy* is that there is no *right of survivorship* in a tenancy in common. When a *tenant in common* dies, his or her share passes according to the terms of any will or other means of passing title to property upon death. Also, *tenants in common* do not have to have equal shares of the property or have the same estate. The court can even partition, or divide, the property if it is in the interests of the tenants as a whole.

Tenancy by the Entirety

A *tenancy by the entirety*, the third type of *concurrent ownership*, can exist only between husband and wife. This tenancy "is created between a husband and wife and by which together they hold title to the whole with *right of survivorship* so that, upon death of either, the other takes whole to the exclusion of deceased heirs." (*Black's Law Dictionary, 5th Edition.*) Like *joint tenancy*, the *four unities* must be satisfied and there is the right of survivorship. It no longer exists in most jurisdictions.

Unlike *joint tenancy, tenancy by the entirety* cannot be severed by a deed drawn by one spouse conveying the property to a third person. The conveyance may be effective, but it will remain subject to the survivorship rights of the other spouse.

A *tenancy by the entirety* cannot be partitioned, but it can be ended. There are three ways in which this can be done: (i) death; (ii) divorce; and (iii) mutual agreement.

Community Property

The fourth form of co-ownership is in *community property*. *Community property* is "property owned in common by husband and wife each having an undivided one-half interest by reason of their marital status." (*Black's Law Dictionary, 5th Edition.*) *Community property* must be acquired during the marriage. Property which is brought to the marriage or received as a gift or an inheritance may be treated as separate property.

Originally, a husband could unilaterally convey the entire property to a third person. Today the signature of both spouses is required. Further, *community property* cannot be severed or partitioned except in the case of divorce or agreement between the parties.

The *right of survivorship* does not apply to community property. A spouse may devise one-half of the property. If there is no will, however, the other spouse will inherit that interest before the heirs.

A recent type of *co-ownership* involves *condominiums*. A *condominium* is a system of separate ownerships of individual units in a multiple-unit building. It is "a single real property parcel with all the unit owners having a right in common to use the common elements with separate ownership confined to the individual units which are serially designated." (*Black's Law Dictionary, 5th Edition.*)

Some *condominium* arrangements involve *time sharing*. *Time sharing* involves ownership of the unit for a certain period of time each year. For the rest of the year, an individual holds a remainder interest in common with the other owners of the same unit.

The fourth way a person may hold or possess property is in a *landlord-tenant relationship*. That interest in land is discussed in the following chapter.

Easements and *covenants running with the land* are discussed later in this book.

HELPFUL HINT #2

REMEMBER

1. A **future estate** does not allow a person holding land to take possession now, but rather in the future.
2. The **possibility of reverter** is a future estate interest retained by the grantor.
3. **Concurrent ownership** occurs when two or more persons share the ownership of some estate in land.
4. There are four requirements necessary for a **joint tenancy**. They are unity of time, title, interest, and possession.
5. The main difference between **tenancy in common** and **joint tenancy** is that there is no right of survivorship in a tenancy in common.

LANDLORD-TENANT

In General

A fourth way a person may hold or possess property is in a *landlord-tenant* relationship. A tenancy involves a conveyance from a landlord, or *lessor*, to the tenant, or *lessee.*

A leasehold is a nonfreehold estate. A nonfreehold estate is said to have a termination date which can be calculated in advance. Therefore, a tenancy is usually set for a specific period of time, whereas a freehold estate ends upon a future event, such as upon death or death without issues or heirs.

When a landlord leases out his or her property, he or she carves an estate out of his or her fee simple and conveys it to the tenant. The landlord, therefore, has a *future interest* and the tenant has a present *possessory estate.* When the tenant is in possession, he or she has all of the possessory rights and privileges of an owner in fee, except for some limitations which will be discussed later.

Types of Tenancies

There are four types of tenancies:

1. Tenancy for years;
2. Periodic tenancy;
3. Tenancy at will; and
4. Tenancy at sufferance.

Tenancy for Years

A *tenancy for years*, also known as a *tenancy for a term*, is a tenancy for a fixed period of time. The beginning and ending dates of the lease period are ascertainable. For example, Stephanie signs a lease which sets forth the following: "The lease is valid for one year from the date of the signing of this lease."

The terms in a *tenancy for years* automatically ends upon the last day of the term. Neither party has to give notice, since termination is automatic. The term can be extended or even shortened, but only by mutual agreement.

A *tenancy for years* is ordinarily created by a written lease. Most states require that if the term is for a year or longer, then the tenancy must be in writing to satisfy the *Statute of Frauds. The Statute of Frauds* is a provision based on an old English statute. It provides that certain contracts must be in writing to be enforceable.

Periodic Tenancy

A *periodic tenancy* is a tenancy for a fixed period of time until the landlord gives notice of termination. Therefore, the period is continuously and automatically renewed unless proper and timely steps to terminate it are taken.

Creation

A *periodic tenancy* can be created either by *express agreement* or *implication.*

Express Agreement

When a *periodic tenancy* is created by *express* agreement, the document explicitly provides for certain terms. For example, a "rental agreement" sets forth a tenancy "from month to month." Again, it is important to remember the *Statute of Frauds* requirement. The writing for a *periodic tenancy* should be in writing when it is long enough to come within the statute.

Implication

A *periodic tenancy* created by *implication* is one where the parties have made no formal agreement regarding a type of tenancy. One person possesses property with the consent of the other and pays rent to the other party. If a lease is invalid, for example, if it fails to comply with the *Statute of Frauds*, but the tenant enters the property and pays rent to the landlord, a *periodic tenancy* may be created.

Remainder After Tenancy has Expired

Similarly, if a tenant remains in possession after the term of his or her tenancy has expired and continues to pay rent to his or her landlord, a *periodic tenancy* may also arise.

Termination

A *periodic tenancy* is terminated when one party gives *timely notice* to the other party with the intent to terminate. Otherwise, the *periodic tenancy* is automatically renewed for the next period.

What is considered *timely notice*? At common law, notice has to be given at least one period in advance (up to six months). Therefore, if the tenancy was "from month to month," then the tenant was required to give one month's notice. This requirement is modified in many jurisdictions by statute.

Tenancy at Will

The third type of tenancy is the *tenancy at will.* A *tenancy at will* lasts only so long as the landlord and tenant desire. It lacks a predetermined termination date. Each is equally capable of terminating the lease at any time.

A tenancy at will is terminated either by *notice* or *implication. A tenancy at will* will be terminated by notice when one party gives notice to the other party. A *tenancy at will* can also be terminated by the death of either party or by a transfer of either party's interest to a third party. These latter events are also referred to as *termination by operation of law.*

Tenancy at Sufferance

The fourth type of tenancy is a *tenancy at sufferance*. Here, the tenant stays over after the expiration of his or her tenancy, but the landlord has not yet taken any eviction action. This tenancy arises when the landlord fails to act. The tenant is not yet a trespasser, even though she entered rightfully and is now there wrongfully.

Right of Possession

The law used to allow a landlord to lease or not lease to whomever he or she pleased for what ever reason he chose. He or she could discriminate based on sex, race, and religion. Two major statutes in this area are the *Civil Rights Act of 1866* and *the Fair Housing Act of 1968.*

Civil Rights Act of 1866

The *Civil Rights Act of 1866* prohibited racial, and only racial, discrimination in the selling and leasing of real and personal property. A plaintiff in such a case could sue the seller or landlord for damages or an injunction.

Fair Housing Act of 1968

The *Fair Housing Act of 1968,* which was an act passed by Congress, went even further. This Act prohibited discrimination in the selling and leasing of property based on race, color, religion, or national origin. Congress amended the act in 1974 to prohibit discrimination based on sex.

At the beginning of the lease term, the landlord must give the tenant the right of possession. If the landlord fails to do so, the landlord is in default. The majority of jurisdictions require the landlord to give the tenant both the *legal right of possession* and *actual possession*. Under the theory of *legal possession*, a tenant has the legal right to occupy the property. *Actual possession* exists where the property is in the immediate occupancy and control of the property. The minority of jurisdictions only require the landlord to deliver the legal right of possession.

Rights and Obligations

Under any lease, both the tenant and landlord have certain rights and obligations. These usually include repair covenants, waste, and remedies.

Waste

At common law, the tenant had a duty to keep the premises in as good a condition for as long as he or she leased it. He or she did not have to make substantial repairs, for example, repairing the roof or repairing the plumbing. However, a tenant was liable for *waste*. Today, a tenant is still liable for *waste*.

There are two types of waste: *ameliorating waste* and *damaging waste.*

Ameliorating Waste

Ameliorating waste is a "change in the physical characteristics of property by an unauthorized act of the tenant or by an act which adds value and improves the property." (*Black's Law Dictionary, 5th Edition.*) An example of *ameliorating waste* is: painting the house or building and addition. Generally, a tenant will not be held liable for this as long as the value of the premises is not lessened.

Damaging Waste

A tenant is liable for *damaging waste* if he or she *substantially* damages the premises. Therefore, a tenant will not be liable for ordinary wear and tear. The damages must extend beyond the term of the lease. Under certain circumstances, a landlord can get an injunction to stop the damage.

Repair Covenants

Most leases contain repair covenants. A covenant by a tenant to repair or to keep the premises in good repair extends beyond that of avoiding waste. It may require him or her to repair damages resulting from any cause.

At common law, a landlord had no duty to put or keep the premises in good repair for the tenant. The landlord's only duty was not to commit fraud, that is misrepresent the condition of the property. Ordinarily, a repair covenant by a landlord will require him or her to make the specified repairs within a reasonable time after receiving notice by the tenant.

Duty to Pay Rent

A tenant also has an affirmative duty to pay his or her rent. Traditionally, the tenant was required to pay his or her rent whether or not the landlord performed his part of the lease. If the value of the rent is not specified, the tenant must pay the reasonable rental value. Most leases require that rent be paid at the beginning of the period, although at common law, rent was due at the end of each period. A landlord can provide for the acceleration of all the unpaid balance of the rent if the tenant breaches the leasing contract.

Some leases require a tenant to pay money in advance to the landlord. The tenant's right to recover this money at the end of the term depends on its characterization. The common forms of advance rental payments are: *security deposits, advance rents,* and *bonuses.*

Implied Warranty of Habitability

As mentioned earlier, at common law the landlord was under no duty to furnish habitable premises. The premises were leased "as is" unless otherwise specified. However, if the landlord knew of defects or dangerous conditions and they were not easily discoverable, the landlord had a duty to disclose the defect. Similarly, if a building was under construction for a particular use and was leased for that use before the completion of construction, a covenant was implied that the building would be fit for that use.

Laws today impose an *implied warranty of habitability*. The standard of habitability has been defined based on housing codes and building codes. A violation of either code which *materially affects* a tenant's health or safety constitutes a violation.

A tenant who is faced with a violation of an *implied warranty of habitability* has a number of options. First, he or she may terminate the lease. Second, he or she may remain on the premises and pay a reduced rate of rent. The reduced rate may be equal to the *actual market rental value* of the premises rather than the rent reserved in the lease. Another formula reduces the amount to the difference between the rental value of the premises "as is" and the rental value it would have been if in the warranted condition. A third formula allows the tenant to reduce the rate by a percentage equal to the degree of livability. A tenant can defend an eviction notice by demonstrating a breach of the *implied warranty of habitability.*

Duty to Injured Tenants and Third Parties

What kind of duty does a landlord owe to tenants and third persons injured on the premises? At common law, the landlord's duty was determined by the visitor's status, ie., trespasser, invitee, etc. Today many jurisdictions treat status as only a factor.

At common law, a landlord was not responsible for defects on the premises. As for subsequent defects, the fact that the tenant was in possession eliminated any duty of the landlord's to enter and repair the defect. If a third person suffered an injury on the premises, their rights were against the possessing tenant and not the landlord.

A number of exceptions have been added to this rule. In fact, they seem to have become more important than the original rule.

Latent Defects

The first exception pertains to *latent defects*. A landlord can be held liable for injuries caused by *latent defects* in the premises which *were known to him or her and disclosed to the tenant*. If the landlord has actual knowledge of a defect in the property, he or she has a duty to speak the truth, but not a duty to inspect. So, the required duty is one of disclosure and not repair.

The failure to disclose also applies to third parties. However, if the landlord has fully disclosed the defect to the tenant, he or she has no duty to the third person. In fact, the tenant is the one who owes a duty of care to his guests.

Common Areas

The second exception refers to *common areas*. A *common area* is the part of the property ". . . over which a landlord retains control (e.g. stairs) and hence for whose condition he is liable." (*Blacks Law Dictionary, 5th Edition.*) Essentially, the landlord is deemed in possession of the *common areas*, while the tenants only have the right of use.

What kind of duty does the landlord owe his or her tenants with respect to the *common areas*? The care owed to his or her tenants is the same as for any possessor of land. Although circumstances may vary, it may include a duty to inspect, to repair, etc. A significant number of courts now hold that a landlord has an obligation to secure *common areas*, such as the doors and windows, from criminal intrusions.

The landlord's duty also extends to third persons and other visitors. They may recover from the landlord if they can show a failure of due care.

Repairs

A third exception to the limited duty of a landlord refers to *repairs*. Although under common law a landlord has no duty to make repairs, if he or she does so, he or she must make those repairs non-negligently. If the landlord performs negligently, he or she will be liable to tenants and third persons, especially if the repair had an appearance of safety.

In addition to *negligent repairs*, a landlord who agrees to make repairs and fails to make them is liable to the cost of repairs and the injuries which result from the disrepair. Most courts extend this *repair rule* to third persons as well. However, even if the tenant did notify his landlord of the defect, he or she may be liable (along with the landlord) to guests for failing to show due care under the circumstances.

Code Compliance

A fourth exception has to do with *code compliance.* Local housing and building codes are imposed on landlords to safeguard the users of the property. These laws are often in the form of *safety statutes and ordinances.* If a landlord violates one of these codes, he or she will be liable for the resulting injuries. Third persons are also protected by these codes and may recover. Again, although these codes impose duties on the landlord and not the tenant, a tenant, nevertheless may be liable to his or her guests if he or she fails to exercise due care towards them.

Exculpatory Clauses

A fifth exception relates to *exculpatory clauses.* Such a clause "...tends to justify, excuse or clear the defendant from alleged fault or guilt." (*Black's Law Dictionary, 5th Edition.*) If a tenant has agreed to repair or to indemnify the landlord for injuries of third parties, this may give the third parties additional rights to recover against him or her for their injuries. However, the tenant and landlord may not agree between themselves that the landlord will not be liable for injuries to other persons who have not entered into that agreement.

Exculpatory clauses are considered void in many jurisdictions as against public policy. They may not be used by a landlord to shield himself or herself against liability that he or she would have under any of the above exceptions.

Lease Transfer

A tenant's interest is a *leasehold interest*. Like any possessory estate, it is fully transferable, unless otherwise provided in the lease.

When a tenant signs a lease, it commonly provides that he or she may not transfer that interest to others without the landlord's consent. Courts generally do not require that a landlord act reasonably with regard to granting or withholding his or her assent to a proposed transfer where consent is required. However, some courts do impose a duty of reasonableness in this situation.

Many leases contain an *anti-assignment clause*. This clause allows the landlord to terminate the tenancy if the tenant attempts to make an improper transfer. However, if a landlord accepts rent after a transfer has been completed, with knowledge of the transfer, he or she generally waives his or her rights to object to the transfer.

There are two forms of lease transfer: *assignments* and *subleases*. Sometimes it can be difficult to distinguish them, but each has different obligations and liabilities.

Assignment

An *assignment* is "a transfer or making over to another of the whole of any property, real or personal, in possession or in action, or of any estate or right therein." (*Black's Law Dictionary, 5th Edition.*)

A tenant transfers his or her entire estate in some or all of the leasehold premises. The *assignee* becomes the new tenant of the landlord. If a tenant transfers only a portion of the premises, there may still be an *assignment*, so long as the *assignee* takes that part for the entire balance of the term.

Even though a tenant who assigns is no longer *in privity of estate* with his landlord, he remains liable if the *assignee* fails to perform, e.g. pay his rent. The landlord can sue the original tenant for the rent if the assignee fails to pay it. Once the original tenant pays the rent, he or she can bring an action against the *assignee*.

To enforce an *assignment*, the landlord must execute a release. The release, which terminates the continuing liability between the original parties, must be an *express release. The assignment* must be more than a promise and it cannot be assumed. Only such an agreement by the landlord can release the tenant from his or her duties to the landlord.

Sublease

A *sublease* is a "transaction whereby tenant grants interests in leased premises less than his own, or reserves to himself reversionary interest in term." (*Black's Law Dictionary, 5th Edition.*) A *sublease* is different from an *assignment* because the tenant who *subleases* is a landlord to his *sublessee*. There is no privity between the original landlord and sublessee. Therefore, neither one can sue the other.

The subtenant is not liable to the landlord for the breach of any covenant. However, if the subtenant fails to perform the covenant, and the tenant also fails to do so, the landlord can terminate the leasehold and the sublease.

A Court's Considerations

Reversion

Courts apply certain rules to determine whether a transfer is an *assignment* or a *sublease*. One of the first things a court may look for is a *reversion*. At common law, if the subleasing tenant conveyed to the sublessee anything less than the whole leasehold estate, it was a *sublease* and not an *assignment*. Similarly, if the new lessee received the whole of the leasehold estate, it was an *assignment* and not a *sublease*.

Right of Entry

Next, a court will examine the *right of entry*. If a transferring tenant retains a *right of entry* and the transferee breaches a condition of the lease, the common law regards the transfer as an *assignment,* not a *sublease.* Most jurisdictions today would hold the transfer as a *sublease.*

Intention of Parties

Because courts recognize the confusion that sometimes occurs with *assignments* and *subleases,* the modern trend is to examine the *intention* of the parties. Courts placing an emphasis on the intent of the parties look at how the parties label the transaction as more important than the duration of the transferee's interest. Therefore, whether the transferee is paying the same or a different amount of rent and whether it is paid to the landlord or to the original tenant are factors which the court will consider in making its final determination.

HELPFUL HINT #3

QUIZ

1. A **tenancy** is usually set for a specific period of time.
   ____T ____F.

2. When a **tenant is in possession**, he or she has all the rights and privileges of an owner in fee. ____T ____F

3. In a **tenancy at will**, the landlord is the only one who may terminate the lease at any time. ____T ____F

4. What is a **tenancy at sufferance**?

Answers

1. True.
2. True.
3. False.
4. When the tenant stays after the expiration of the tenancy without the landlord's consent.

HELPFUL HINT #4

Discussion

1. Discuss some examples of **standards of habitability.**
2. Discuss the process of **disclosure** of defects and how this affects landlord and tenant liability.
3. Discuss the **landlord's rights** in a sublease situation.

EASEMENTS

In General

An *easement* is "a right of use over the property of another." (*Black's Law Dictionary, 5th Edition.*) This chapter will familiarize you with the terminology and nature of easements. It will introduce you to the characteristics of *easements* and discuss how *easements* are created. This chapter will also examine the various types of *easements*, how they can be *enforced, transferred* and *subdivided*. The final section of this chapter will deal with how *easements* are terminated.

Characteristics of Easements

To begin, a parcel of land which is subject to an *easement* is called a *servient tenement. A servient tenement* is "an estate in respect of which a service is owing, as the dominant tenement is that to which the service is due." (*Black's Law Dictionary, 5th Edition.*) The owner or possessor of a *servient tenement* is the *servient tenant.*

A parcel of land which is benefitted by an *easement* is referred to as the *dominant tenement. A dominant tenement* is "that to which a servitude or easement is due, or for the benefit of which it exists." (*Black's Law Dictionary, 5th Edition.*) The owner or possessor of a *dominant tenement* is the *dominant tenant.*

An *easement* is called *appurtenant* when it benefits the land. In other words ". . . when it is by right used with the land for its benefit, as in the case of a way, or water-course, or of a passage for light, air, or heat from across the land of another" (*Black's Law Dictionary, 5th Edition*), it will be *appurtenant.*

For example, Roger (the servient tenant) granted Louise (the dominant tenant) "the right to walk over my property to get from your house to the road." In this example, Louise's *easement* is *appurtenant*, since the privilege of crossing Roger's property benefits her in her capacity as possessor of her house.

On the other hand, an *easement* will be *in gross* when it benefits a person. In that case, there is no *dominant tenement* but there is always a *servient tenement.* Sometimes it is difficult to determine if an *easement* is *appurtenant* or *in gross.* Technically, for land to be *appurtenant,* an *easement* must be intended to, and must, in fact, benefit a person with regard to his or her possession. Despite this requirement, courts prefer to find an easement *appurtenant.*

Sometimes the use of land allows for the removal of some product from the soil, for example, oil or minerals. This interest is referred to as *profit*. It is "the benefit, advantage, or pecuniary gain accruing to the owner or occupant of land from its actual use ..." (*Black's Law Dictionary, 5th Edition.*)

When the use of the *easement* is revocable at the will of the *servient tenant*, it is referred to as a *license*. For example, King says to Paul, "You can park your mobile home on my lot until I tell you to move it." Paul has a *license*, a *revocable non-possessory interest* in King's land.

Once you have identified the *servient* and *dominant tenements*, it is also important to determine if an *easement* is an *affirmative easement* or a *negative easement*.

An *affirmative easement* permits the dominant tenant to do acts affecting the servient land which would otherwise be unprivileged.

A *negative easement* gives the *dominant tenant* the right to prevent the *servient tenant* from doing acts affecting the servient land which would otherwise be privileged. For example, Loretta granted Joe "an easement of view over my property." Joe has a *negative easement. The easement* involves the right to stop Loretta from building on her own land, which she would otherwise be free, or privileged, to do.

Creating Easements

Now that we have identified some of the basic characteristics of *easements*, let us examine how *easements* can be created. Basically, there are three ways in which an *easement* can be created:

1. Express language;
2. Implication; and
3. Prescription.

Express Language

An *easement* can be created by express language in a deed. A *deed* is an instrument for creating an easement. An *easement* will be created if a *deed is from servient to dominant tenement, or conveys other property to the dominant tenant*. A deed can also grant an *easement* in the property granted.

There is no specific language which must be included in the deed, but it must not be ambiguous. A court must be able to determine that some kind of possessory estate has been created with restrictions.

Generally, the *Statute of Frauds* requires that there be a writing. An exception is made in most cases for *easements* of less than a year.

An *easement* made by oral grant usually creates a *license*. However, if a *grantee* relies to his or her detriment on the oral grant, it may be viewed not as a *license*, but as an *easement*.

Easement by Implication

The second way in which an *easement* can be created is by *implication*. When someone conveys a property interest, a court may imply from the circumstances that the parties also intended to grant or reserve an *easement* as well. A court will determine that an *implied easement* exists if, by inference, the original parties would have added language to the deed granting or reserving the *easement* if they had thought about it.

A court will take into consideration a number of factors in determining if an *easement* is implied. For example, a partial conveyance will establish the foundation for the implication that the parties intended to benefit one of the parcels at the expense of the other.

In order for an *easement* to be implied, there must be *prior use*. This implication is based on the assumption that the parties intended the preexisting use to continue even though it was not written in a deed.

The *prior use* must be *apparent* or at least *discoverable upon reasonable inspection*. Rights-of-way and other features described on a map may be proof enough of *prior use*, despite the lack of express granting language in the deeds.

The *easement* must be a necessity. In other words, the *easement* must furnish a *significant benefit to the claimed dominant tenant*. If necessity cannot be shown, a court will not imply the existence of an *easement* against the alleged *servient tenant*. It is important to note that when there is an *absolute necessity, an easement* will be implied, whether or not there was any *prior use*. This implication is based on public policy notions rather than the *intent of the parties. An easement by necessity* exists only so long as the necessity exists.

Easement by Prescription

The third way in which an *easement* can be created is by *prescription. An easement is created by prescription* when the use has been "...open, continuous, exclusive, and under claim of right for statutory period." (*Black's Law Dictionary, 5th Edition.*) To this extent, it resembles *adverse possession*. However, it differs in that the adverse user acquires only an easement and not title. As with *adverse possession*, the *adverse requirement means non-permissiveness and not necessarily animosity.*

The adverse use does not have to be *exclusive*. Remember, exclusivity is a characteristic of possession, but not use. An *adverse possessor* must have been in *exclusive possession for the entire statutory period*. An adverse user need not prohibit others from using the property, so long as their use does not interfere with his or her use.

The use must be *uninterrupted*. An interruption only occurs when the possessor actually blocks the adverse user. Therefore, simultaneous use by the possessor does not necessarily interrupt a *prescriptive use*.

For example, Jana walks across the same path as Kevin, but she does not interrupt his use. Jana must put up some kind of barrier or bring a suit against Kevin to stop the statutory period from running.

The adverse use must be *continuous*. It will be *continuous* so long as it is regular and more than occasional. Therefore, *seasonal adverse use* may be sufficient to acquire a *prescriptive easement*.

Rights in Easements

Easements often entitle the holder to various limited rights and privileges in property. Courts are often called upon to determine the extent of those interests.

Express Easement

In an *express easement*, the language is the controlling determinant of its holder's activities. A grant or reservation that is explicit as to certain activities must be followed as prescribed. If an *easement* is silent as to other features, courts will "fill the gaps." The court will make its ruling on the basis that the *easement* is not unreasonably burdensome.

What kinds of elements factor into the reasonableness of the *easement*? The court will consider whether an activity occurred prior to the creation of the *easement*, whether there was an objection after the *easement's* creation, the actual purpose of the easement, and if any consideration was paid for the use of the *easement*. Courts also assume that the parties contemplated a normal development of the *dominant tenement* over time. Therefore, courts permit changes in relation to that development.

Implied Easement

In an *implied easement*, there is no express language to aid in construction of the *easement*. The court looks at the same factors in determining the scope of the *easement* as it does when it determines if the *easement* exists.

For example, when Corrine sold her house and stable to Floyd, a path ran from the stable over the land to the main street. An *easement* arose by implication and its scope permitted Floyd to ride his horse across the trail. Cars have generally replaced horses, and the stable has become a garage. Floyd may be allowed to drive across the same trail.

Prescriptive Easement

In a *prescriptive easement*, the pattern of the original use determines what other uses will be permitted. Generally, a *servient tenant* who did not sue when the original adverse use occurred would also have tolerated similar use.

The *dominant tenant* is obliged to keep the *easement* in repair. The *servient tenant* has no repair obligations. However, as long as he or she possesses the property, he or she may be liable in tort for disrepair. Further, either party that conducts any unreasonable activity relating to the *easement* may *enjoin*, or require to stop, that activity. Extreme abuses may extinguish the use of the *easement* entirely.

Transferring or Dividing Easements

So far, we have examined the characteristics of *easements*, how they are created, and the scope of their interests. We will now discuss how *easements* can be transferred or divided.

Transferability

Parties who create the *easement* can be as specific as they want as to its transferability. An *easement* that is silent will have to follow a few extra rules.

One element which the parties will have to consider is the *burden of the easement. The burden of an easement is not separable from the servient land.* The transfer of the *burden of an easement* refers to the transfer of the land subject to it.

A *transfer will affect the burden of the easement.* Once the servient tenement is conveyed or leased, the transferee becomes the new servient tenant.

Subdividing

A *subdivision* will also affect the burden of the *easement.* If a *servient estate* is subdivided, each new parcel is subject to the *easement.* However, if it is located in such an area where it will apply to only some parts of the *servient land*, the other parts are no longer servient.

For example, Ross' property is subject to a right-of-way *easement* that runs east and west across the northern edge of his property. If he sells the property, the new owner takes the land subject to the easement. If Ross subdivides his property in a north and south parcel, then the south parcel is free from the *easement.*

In addition to taking into consideration the *burden of the easement*, the parties will also have to take into consideration the *benefit of the easement*. It is possible to transfer the *benefit* without transferring the *dominant tenement.*

A transfer of the *dominant tenement* carries with it all incidental benefits, including *easements appurtenant*. The new grantee of a *dominant tenement* automatically becomes the new *dominant tenant.*

At common law, *an easement* or *a profit in gross* could not be subdivided or transferred. The more modern view permits exceptions in both cases. *Easements* can be transferred when they are commercial. Also, some jurisdictions allow *easements* to be subdivided when they are quantifiable, for example when a person has the right to make only ten trips a day over a road, or when some royalty is being paid.

TERMINATING AN EASEMENT

The final section of this chapter discusses how an easement is terminated. There are five major methods:

1. Natural duration;
2. Merger;
3. Release and abandonment;
4. Prescription; and
5. Forfeiture.

Natural Duration

The first way in which an *easement* can be terminated is by *natural duration*. For example, if an *easement* is created for only a limited period of time, it terminates once the time passes. Generally, an *easement* is considered a *fee simple*, unless otherwise indicated.

Merger

The second way in which an *easement* can be terminated is by *merger*. In a *merger, a dominant tenant acquires the servient estate, or vice versa*. The interests are merged, and the *easement* is terminated.

Release and Abandonment

The third way in which an *easement* can be terminated is by *release and abandonment*. Under this theory, *a dominant tenant may convey his or her easement to the servient tenant and the easement will merge into the servient estate and be destroyed.*

The *easement* must be transferred by deed or by an oral statement of release accompanied with extended nonuse or conduct which demonstrates an intent to abandon the *easement*. An oral release is ineffective.

Prescription

The fourth way in which an *easement* can be terminated is by *prescription*. If a servient tenant *unreasonably interferes with an easement, the dominant tenant* may sue. If he or she fails to bring suit within the statutory period, he or she loses the right to sue and therefore loses the *easement*.

Forfeiture

The final way in which an *easement* can be terminated is by *forfeiture*. This is done pursuant to a judicial decree, usually when a *dominant tenant abuses an easement*.

HELPFUL HINT #5

DEFINITIONS

1. **EASEMENT**: A right to use the property of another.
2. **SERVIENT TENEMENT**: A parcel of land which is subject to an easement.
3. **DOMINANT TENEMENT**: A parcel of land which is benefitted by an easement.
4. **EXPRESS EASEMENT:** An easement that uses language to control its holder's activities.

HELPFUL HINT #6

REMEMBER

1. In an **implied easement**, there is no express language to aid in the construction of the easement.

2. In a **prescriptive easement**, the pattern of the original use determines what other uses will be permitted.

3. Parties who create the **easement** can be as specific as they want as to its transferability.

4. There are five major methods to **terminate** an easement. They are: natural duration, merger, release and abandonment, prescription, and forfeiture.

COVENANTS RUNNING WITH THE LAND

In General

A *covenant running with the land* is "a covenant which goes with the land, as being annexed to the estate, and which cannot be separated from the land, and transferred without it." (*Black's Law Dictionary, 5th Edition.*) It can be enforced not only against the original parties but also against the successors of either party.

This chapter will describe the nature of *covenants*, their elements, the scope of their interest, and how they can be terminated.

Before discussing the requirements of a *covenant*, we should make the distinction between *easements* and *covenants*. They are often confused.

In an *easement, a servient tenant* can transfer no more than he or she has; thus the burden of the *easement* is *automatically transferred* to every successive owner of the servient estate. If the *easement* is *appurtenant*, its benefit is automatically transferred along with any transfer of the *dominant estate.*

Covenants are created by promissory language, such as "I promise." Easements are created from conveyancing terminology, such as, "I grant." Courts do not always adhere to the fine-line distinctions in this technical language.

Requirements

In order for a *covenant to run with the land*, a number of requirements must be met.

First, no *covenant will run with the land* unless it is enforceable as between the original parties. This means that it must not violate any contract principles or other applicable laws.

Since a *covenant running with the land* inherently involves the land, the *Statute of Frauds* requires that it be in writing and signed by the party to be charged.

In addition to the requirement that the covenant satisfy any legal requirements, the covenant must reflect the original parties' *intent to create a covenant running with the land.* At common law the intent to create a *covenant running with the land had to be expressed through the word "assigns."* Today, most courts do no require any special terminology.

Some jurisdictions distinguish between *covenants at law* and *covenants in equity.* The rules governing covenants at law were established in 1583, while the rules in equity did not develop until over 200 years later.

Covenants at Law

There are three requirements for a *covenant at law*. A covenant at law must:

1. Touch and concern the land;
2. Satisfy the requirement of privity of estate; and
3. Include succession to the entire estate.

Touch and Concern

The only covenants which may *run with the land* are those which relate to the land. This requirement is expressed in the theory that the *covenant must touch and concern the land.* Two aspects of the *touch and concern* requirement are *benefit* and *burden*. Every promise involves a *burden* imposed upon the promisor and a *benefit* gained by the promisee or third person.

The *burden of a covenant touches and concerns land* if it affects the covenantor in his or her capacity as owner or possessor. If the *covenantor* is inhibited from doing something on his or her land, in a manner which he or she would otherwise be free to do, then the *burden touches and concerns the land.* This is known as a *negative covenant.*

If the activity which the covenantor agrees to undertake occurs on his or her own property and is something that he or she would not otherwise be required to do, then the burden of his or her promise *touches and concerns the land.* This is referred to as an *affirmative covenant.*

The benefit of a covenant touches and concerns the land if it increases the covenantee's use or enjoyment of his or her land. This usually means that the land has become more valuable.

Sometimes a promise may contain a *burden which touches and concerns land while its benefit does not do so, or vice versa.* For example, if Jeremy promises not to engage in a certain activity on his land that he otherwise would be privileged to do and which would compete with the activity of Lara on her property, the *burden touches and concerns the land.* However, some courts hold that the *benefit* of this promise does not *touch and concern* Lara's land; it increases the commercial value of her business, but it does not relate to her use and enjoyment of the property.

Courts are not in agreement as to when the *burden or the benefit touches and concerns the land.* Some courts take a liberal view, requiring only that the side involved *touch and concern land* in order to run. A stricter view requires that the burden of a *covenant will not run with the land unless both it and the benefit of the covenant touch and concern the land.*

Privity of Estate

The second requirement for a *covenant at law* is *privity of estate*, also referred to as *horizontal privity*. A number of states require that the original parties to the covenant be involved in a special relationship at the time the covenant is made.

States are not in agreement as to what relationships satisfy this requirement. The strictest version of this privity requirement involves *leases*. In a lease, privity means tenure. Only covenants in leases can run under this standard. Less restrictive views recognize privity in *shared* interests, as between co-owners and *conveyances by deed.*

Succession to the Entire Estate

The third requirement for a *covenant at law* is one that a number of states recognize. These jurisdictions hold that the *burden of a covenant* runs only to persons who succeed to the entire estate of the covenantor.

Covenants in Equity

There are three requirements for *covenants in equity.* The system of equity was developed for plaintiffs who desired *injunctive rather than monetary relief*. The requirements are as follows:

1. Touch and concern;
2. Horizontal and vertical privity;
3. Notice.

Touch and Concern

The first requirement is that the *covenant touch and concern the land. No burden of a covenant will run, either at law or in equity, if it does not touch and concern the land, nor will any benefit run if it does not touch and concern the land.*

Horizontal Privity and Vertical Privity

There are also *horizontal privity* and *vertical privity* requirements. *Horizontal privity* is not required for *covenants in equity*. Thus covenants between neighbors may be enforced in equity by and against their successors. Similarly, *easement burdens and benefits run to all subsequent possessors of the servient and dominant tenements.* Thus a tenant of the covenantor is bound or benefitted in equity by the covenant.

Notice

Finally, there is a *notice* requirement. At law, a *covenant runs with the land* whether or not the successor has notice of it. However, *equitable easements* can only be created when it is equitable to do so. These covenants are often subject to recording acts.

SUBDIVISION

So far, we have discussed the nature and requirements of a *covenant running with the land*. We will now discuss how a *covenant running with the land* can be subdivided.

Subdivisions usually occur in a situation where a developer wants to regulate architectural layout and maintenance. An example of a subdivision is illustrated in either a condominium or cooperative.

The developer is usually the original promisee of all the covenants made by the individual purchasers. Typically, once the land is completed, the developer is not interested in maintaining any connection with the *subdivisions*. Rather, he creates a homeowners association and turns over the enforcement of any covenants to the association.

Each *subdivision* owner may enforce a *covenant* against any other lot owner who also took a deed from the developer at a later time. This theory is based on the fact that the *covenant* in the deed benefitted all of the developer's retained land and ran with the land when it was conveyed.

This enforcement against neighbors does not apply to later purchasers in the subdivision who took their deeds from individual owners in the subdivision who themselves had preceded the covenantor. Land which was previously conveyed away by the subdivider cannot be directly benefitted by a covenant later made to him.

This subsequently acquired land is generally not treated as benefitted by the *covenant*, and the purchasers of those parcels cannot enforce it against the original covenantor.

Prior owners have a more difficult time enforcing restrictions against subsequent grantees. However, there are some theories that can alleviate this problem.

For example, if a developer promised one purchaser he would impose restrictions upon all the rest of his land as he sold it, all the remaining land would become subject to a burden for the benefit of the one special lot. For example, Joseph conveyed Lot 1 to Craig, inserting in his deed that all the other land would be restricted to residential uses. Joseph then conveyed Lot 2 to Anika, without imposing such a restriction. In such a case, Craig or any of his successors may prohibit Anika from engaging in any commercial activity on the ground that Lot 2 became subject to the burden of Joseph's *covenant* with Lot 1.

Termination of Covenants

Our discussion of *covenants* will now turn to how a *covenant running with the land is terminated.*

Legal Defenses

There are five legal defenses for the termination of a *covenant*:

1. Pursuant to the creating document;
2. Pursuant to a statute;
3. Merger;
4. Release; and
5. Abandonment.

The creating document itself may limit the life of the *covenant*. Some condominiums have *renewal provisions* in their restrictions, which require a certain vote by the homeowners after a fixed number of years.

Some *covenants* are limited by *statute* and will override any inconsistent time period prescribed in the document creating the *covenant*.

Still other *covenants* are terminated by a *merger of the benefitted and burdened estates under one ownership*. A party benefitted by a covenant may release the burdened party. However, this is subject to joint release if other parties are involved.

Finally, a *covenant* may be terminated by *abandonment*. This will occur in two situations. In one situation, the developer has abandoned his scheme of inserting a particular *covenant* in his later deeds which he had placed in his earlier deeds. Abandonment also occurs if violations of the owners are so widespread within a subdivision that there is no longer any general plan in effect.

Equitable Defenses

In addition to the legal defenses for the termination of *covenants*, there are also four equitable defenses. They are:

1. Changed conditions;
2. Unclean hands;
3. Acquiescence; and
4. Laches.

Changed Conditions

The first equitable defense is *changed conditions*. If, for example, a neighborhood has changed so much that enforcement will unfairly oppress the defendant and not achieve any significant advantage for the plaintiff, the court will not compel obedience to the restriction.

Unclean Hands

The second equitable defense is the theory of *unclean hands*. If the plaintiff seeking to enforce a *covenant* has already breached it himself or herself, it is not likely that a court will permit him or her to enforce it against another.

Acquiescence

The third equitable defense is that of *acquiescence*. If the plaintiff has tolerated similar breaches by other owners, he or she may be prohibited from enforcing it against the next owner. This defense is not applicable if the previously tolerated breaches have not substantially affected an owner's property.

Laches

The fourth equitable defense is that of *laches*. The doctrine of laches "...is based upon the maxim that equity aids the vigilant, and not those who slumber on their rights." (*Black's Law Dictionary, 5th Edition.*) Generally, if a person for an *unreasonable and unexplained* length of time neglects or admits to assert his or her right, he or she in effect *abandons or waives* his or her right or claim.

Governmental Intervention

A *covenant* may be affected if the government intervenes and initiates an *eminent domain* proceeding. *Eminent domain* is "the power to take private property for public use by the state, municipalities, and private persons or corporations authorized to exercise functions of public character." (*Black's Law Dictionary, 5th Edition.*) Most courts today require the government to compensate the parties for their loss.

The government may also take over property if the owner fails to pay the taxes due on it. However, courts are divided as to whether or not the person who buys it at the government tax sale takes the property subject to the burdens of the *covenants* or free of them.

HELPFUL HINT #7

QUIZ

1. A **covenant running with the land** may be enforced against__________________ and ____________________.

2. **Covenants** are created by__________________ language.

3. What are the three requirements for a **covenant at law**?

4. The system of **covenants in equity** was developed for parties who desired __________________ relief rather than ___________________ relief.

ANSWERS

1. The original parties are the successors of either party.
2. Promissory.
3. Touch and concern the land, privity of estate and succession to the entire estate.
4. Injunctive, Monetary.

HELPFUL HINT #8

Discussion

1. Discuss the **five legal defenses** for the **termination** of a covenant.

2. Discuss the **four equitable defenses** for the **termination** of covenants.

CONVEYANCING: THE SALE AND TRANSFER OF LAND

IN GENERAL

This chapter will examine contracts for the sale of land. Generally, under the *Statute of Frauds*, a written contract is required in the sale and purchase of land. The contract must contain certain criteria and provisions specific to the parties and property. It is also important that property have *marketable title*. *Marketable title* refers to property which is free of encumbrances and reasonable doubt as to its validity. There are a number of situations which affect the conveyance of real property. For example, the doctrine of *equitable conversion* applies in situations where a death intervenes with the signing of an agreement to sell real property. The buyer, seller, and vendor all have obligations in the conveyance of real property.

Contract for the Sale of Real Property - Requirements

What makes a contract enforceable in the sale and purchase of real property? There are five basic requirements:

1. Parties' intent to be bound;
2. Legal consideration;
3. Writing;
4. Time for performance; and
5. Risk provisions.

Intent to be Bound

In order for a contract to exist between two parties, there must be a *mutual intent to be bound*. When an owner tells his or her broker to list his or her property for sale, this does not constitute an offer to sell it. Rather, it is only an agreement allowing the broker to find a purchaser. The owner has the authority to reject any offer from a potential buyer even if the offer conforms exactly to the seller's terms. The owner may have to pay the broker's commission under the listing agreement, but the owner is not required to sell his or her property until he or she actually accepts an offer.

Legal Consideration

The second requirement which makes a contract for the sale of real property enforceable is *legal consideration.* In other words, the seller's promise to convey his or her property must be satisfied by the buyer's promise to pay the seller's price.

For a contract to be enforceable it cannot be *illusory.* An *illusory promise* is "a purported promise that actually promises nothing because it leaves to the speaker the choice of performance or nonperformance." (*Black's Law Dictionary, 5th Edition.*) Essentially, if a promise is illusory, there is no requirement for the promisor to act, so if accepted, the promisee may receive nothing.

In a situation in which a buyer's obligation to pay is dependent upon his or her satisfaction with some feature of the property, such as zoning approval, or if the seller's obligation to sell the property is dependent upon his or her satisfaction of the payment, the satisfaction of such clauses will either be based on an *objective* reading by the court (the *reasonable person standard*) or a *subjective* reading (*good faith*) into the provision. Such personal satisfaction contracts are not illusory. A promise, such as "I will sell you my property if I feel like it in the morning," is illusory because there is no definite committment.

The Writing

A third requirement to make a contract for the sale of land enforceable is the *writing*. The *Statute of Frauds* requires that a contract for the sale of land be in writing and signed by the party to be charged. The writing itself must contain a number of standard provisions.

1. Description of the land;
2. Names of the parties;

3. Price;
4. Time for performance; and
5. Risk provisions.

Description of the Land

The writing must include a description of the land to be conveyed. A full legal description which includes specific measurements is not required. An informal description which includes the street address will suffice, as long as it will properly identify the property.

Names of the Parties

The writing must also include the names of the parties. Both the buyer and seller must be identified. The buyer may designate that his or her right to purchase can be taken by a "nominee." This arrangement is generally acceptable so long as he or she remains bound to perform the obligations set forth in the contract.

Price

A third element found in a writing is the *price*. Generally, a contract must specify the price to be paid. However, in some jurisdictions, a contract will simply call for a reasonable price. The method of payment does not have to be specified in the contract, but if it is silent on this matter, the court will assume that the price is to be paid in all cash at the time of conveyance.

When a contract has to be modified or revoked for one reason or another, many jurisdictions do not require it to be in writing. The *Statute of Frauds* only applies to the initial creation of the contract. Subsequent changes can be made orally.

A court will also enforce a writing for the sale of real property if it is *partly performed*. There are a variety of situations which constitute *part performance*. For instance, if the property has been transferred to the buyer or if the buyer has paid part of the sale price and is now in possession.

Time for Performance

The fourth requirement for the enforcement of a contract for real property is *time for performance.* Generally, a contract does not have to specify the exact date of performance in which the parties must act. If no such date is expressed, a court will imply that the transaction be performed within a *reasonable time.*

Where a contract does set a day for exact performance, the court treats that term as an *essential term.* Courts will not excuse belated performance by either party. However, a court will excuse a party if the delay can be compensated. The court will not grant the excuse if the contract specifically states that *time is of the essence.*

Risk Provisions

The fifth requirement in a contract for the sale of real property is the description of the various *risk provisions.* These provisions deal with the allocation of income and expenses during the contract period (for example, taxes and insurance), the risk of physical destruction before the settlement, the kind of payment required, and remedies for breach of the contract.

Marketable Title

Marketable title is ". . . one which is free from reasonable doubt and will not expose the party who holds it to hazards of litigation." (*Black's Law Dictionary, 5th Edition.*) *Marketable title* is title which is not subject to encumbrances such as back taxes, easements, covenants, and leases. It is title which an informed, prudent and reasonable purchaser would be willing to accept as performance of the contract.

Elements

What kinds of elements factor into a title's marketability? First, consider if the buyer possesses the *entire estate*. If he or she only owns a fractional interest, such as a *tenant in common*, the title is unmarketable unless the contract itself calls for the lesser interest.

Marketable title also includes a complete and accurate *chain of title. A chain of title* is the "successive conveyances, or other forms of alienation, affecting a particular parcel of land, arranged consecutively, from the government or original source of title down to the present holder." (*Black's Law Dictionary, 5th Edition.*) A court may declare title unmarketable when there is a significant discrepancy in the spelling of a name, a boundary discrepancy, or a defective document.

Restrictions

Whenever there are monetary burdens, such as back taxes or tax liens, the seller can usually utilize the purchase price to satisfy mortgage or tax liens on the title to convey title free of any claims to the buyer.

The escrow agent will take part of the funds which are deposited by the buyer and pay them to the lien holders rather than the seller, in order to satisfy and remove the liens from the title.

Zoning and subdivision restrictions often do not affect the marketability of title. A buyer cannot complain about title simply because it is subject to an ordinance. However, existing violations of land-use ordinances often make the title unmarketable.

Generally, *physical defects* to the property do not affect marketability of title. Thus, title may even be marketable if structures are termite infested. Building code violations may affect title if the city has instituted any kind of action to abate the situation.

Marketable title is implied in every land sale contract. This means that the buyer is entitled to insist that the purchase will be subject to that condition.

Consequences

What happens in the event title is not marketable? The consequences are different based on whether it is *prior to closing, at closing, or after closing.*

A seller has no obligation to have *marketable title prior to the date set for performance.* Title must be marketable only when the deed is tendered. The seller may use the funds received from the buyer towards clearing the title.

If title is not marketable on the *closing date*, the buyer may withdraw from the contract and/or seek judicial relief. Sometimes a seller is allowed a reasonable time after the closing date to *cure* defects in title if the contract does not make *time of the essence.*

Once the buyer accepts the seller's deed, the buyer's obligation regarding marketable title is satisfied. If the title is defective, then the buyer's claim is dependent upon his or her rights under the contract. These rights may be subject to provisions that survive the closing.

Equitable Conversions

Now that we have discussed the requirements of real property contracts and the nature of marketable title, we can examine *equitable conversions.*

The doctrine of equitable conversion is "a doctrine commonly applied when death intervenes between the signing of an agreement to sell real estate and the date of transfer of title resulting in treating land as personalty and takes place when a contract for the sale of realty becomes binding on parties." (*Black's Law Dictionary, 5th Edition.*)

Equitable conversion will not apply unless the buyer has exercised his or her option to purchase the property. He or she will not be entitled to take the property until legal title has been transferred to him or her unless the seller permits him or her to enter. Therefore, *equitable conversion* affects title, not possession. After the title has been transferred, the seller's creditors may be able to reach the balance of the price owned by the buyer, but not the title to the land. On the other hand, the buyer's creditors may be able to reach the title.

Risk of Loss

Before a contract is executed, all risk of loss from destruction of the property not caused by any party is upon the seller. When the contract is executed and the buyer is the full owner, the buyer bears the *risk of loss*. Courts are not in agreement as to who bears the risk during the contract period.

The *majority* of courts hold that the buyer bears the loss. The buyer must pay the full price even when the premises have been totally destroyed prior to the close of escrow.

The *minority* of courts hold that the seller bears the loss. This is based on the theory that there is an implied condition in the contract that the premises will be transferred to the buyer in the condition they were in when the contract was first made.

Neither of these rules apply if the parties have specifically provided for a different risk allocation in their contract.

The contract between the buyer and seller is formed when the seller delivers a deed to the buyer and the buyer pays the full price to the seller. If the price is not all cash, a mortgage may be involved.

Further, when the contract has been completed, the rights of the parties are no longer governed by the contract. Their legal relationship, thereafter, will depend on *fraud* or *warranty.*

Fraud is "an intentional perversion of truth for the purpose of inducing another in reliance upon it to part with some valuable thing belonging to him or to surrender a legal right." (*Black's Law Dictionary, 5th Edition.*)

A *Warranty* is "a promise that a proposition of fact is true." (*Black's Law Dictionary, 5th Edition.*)

BREACH

What happens if either the buyer or seller breaches the contract? What are their respective rights?

Seller's Breach

If the seller fails or refuses to convey the property at closing, the buyer can *withdraw* from the contact, seek *specific performance,* or *sue for damages.* However, if the seller's performance is delayed because of a need to clear title defects, the buyer may be required to wait a *reasonable time* before canceling.

Specific performance is granted only in extreme cases. Since land is considered unique, *specific performance* may be granted only under certain circumstances. For example, if the seller's title is unmarketable, but the defects are merely technical, the buyer may be granted *specific performance.*

When the seller breaches the contract, the buyer may sue to recover his deposit and out-of-pocket expenses.

Buyer's Breach

If the buyer breaches and fails to pay the purchase price, the seller may also seek *specific performance, sue for damages,* or *withdraw* from the contract.

A decree of *specific performance* will order the buyer to pay the purchase price and convey the title to the buyer.

If the seller wants to collect damages, the contract may provide for *liquidated damages*. The contract may also allow the seller to retain the deposit if the buyer defaults. These damages must be reasonable. If *liquidated damages* are not allowed, the seller may recover the difference between the *selling price* and *market value of the property.*

The seller may also terminate the contract. He may attempt to resell the property elsewhere for a greater profit or he may return the buyer's deposit, less his out-of-pocket expenses.

CONVEYANCES OF LAND

In General

A *conveyance* is "an instrument by which some estate or interest in land is transferred from one person to another; such as a deed, mortgage, etc." (*Black's Law Dictionary, 5th Edition.*)

A *deed* is the usual instrument for conveying property. Title passes when a *deed has been properly executed and delivered.* It is important to note that a *deed* is not title; it is merely the instrument for *transferring* title.

The *Statute of Frauds* requires that any transfer in the interest of land be in writing. Therefore, a deed must be in writing.

Writing Requirements

There are four basic requirements which must be included in a deed:

1. Identification of the parties;
2. Intent to convey;
3. Interest of land being conveyed; and
4. Description of the land.

Identification of the Parties

The actual writing requires the identification of the *grantee*, the "one to whom a grant is made." (*Black's Law Dictionary, 5th Edition.*) It also requires the signature of the *grantor*, "the person by whom a grant is made." (*Black's Law Dictionary, 5th Edition.*)

Intent to Convey

The writing must also indicate an intent by the *grantor* to convey her interest. Ordinarily the word "grant" or "convey" is used. However, no technical words are necessary.

Interest of Land Being Conveyed

The writing must indicate the interest of land being conveyed. Unless otherwise stated, it is presumed that the *grantor* is conveying the entire interest.

Description of the Land

Finally, the deed must describe the land being conveyed. One way of describing land is by *metes and bounds. Metes and bounds* are "the boundary lines of land, with their terminal points and angles." (*Black's Law Dictionary, 5th Edition.*)

Another way of describing the property is by *monument. Monuments* are "visible marks or indications left on natural or other objects indicating the lines and boundaries of a survey." (*Black's Law Dictionary, 5th Edition.*) It often includes pillars, posts, stone markers, and natural objects such as blazed trees and water courses.

Where a river or stream constitutes a boundary, boundary lines are subject to *accretion and reliction,* and *avulsion.*

Consider the situation where neighbors share the same stream. *Accretion* occurs when the land which separates them adds to one side. *Reliction* occurs when the land is removed from the other side to conform to the new course of the water. *Avulsion*, which is the sudden and dramatic change to the land caused by water, does not change boundary lines.

TYPES OF DEEDS

There are three types of deeds. They are distinguished by the representations made by the grantor concerning the state of title. The three deeds are:

1. Quitclaim deed;
2. Statutory deed; and
3. Warranty deed.

Quitclaim Deed

A *quitclaim deed* makes no representations concerning the state of the grantor's title. It is a deed that is "...intended to pass any title, interest, or claim which the grantor may have in the premises, but not professing that such title is valid, nor containing any warranty or covenants for title." (*Black's Law Dictionary, 5th Edition.*)

Statutory Deed

Some jurisdictions provide statutes that create limited covenants. Some of these limited covenants provide that the grantor has not previously conveyed the estate, or that the grantor has not personally allowed any encumbrances to be placed against the title.

Warranty Deed

A *warranty deed* is a "deed in which grantor warrants good clear title." (*Black's Law Dictionary, 5th Edition.*) This type of deed contains six statements by the grantor concerning the title of the property. The first three are *present covenants* and the second three are *future covenants.*

1. Covenant of seisin;
2. Covenant of right to convey;
3. Covenant against encumbrances;
4. Covenant of quiet enjoyment;
5. Covenant of warranty; and
6. Covenant of further assurances.

Covenant of Seisin

Covenant of seisin is "an assurance to the purchaser that the grantor has the very same estate in quantity and quality which he purports to convey." (*Black's Law Dictionary, 5th Edition.*)

Covenant of Right to Convey

The *covenant of right to convey* is "an assurance by the covenantor that the grantor has sufficient capacity and title to convey the estate which he by his deed undertakes to convey." (*Black's Law Dictionary, 5th Edition.*)

Covenant Against Encumbrances

The *covenant against encumbrances* is "a covenant that there are no incumbrance on the land conveyed." (*Black's Law Dictionary, 5th Edition.*) Encumbrances would include, for example, easements and mortgages.

Covenant of Quiet Enjoyment

The *covenant of quiet enjoyment* is a covenant which states that the grantee will be able to quietly enjoy the property against lawful claims by any third parties.

Covenant of Warranty

The *covenant of warranty* is "an assurance by the grantor of an estate that the grantee shall enjoy the same without interruption by virtue of paramount title." (*Black's Law Dictionary, 5th Edition.*)

Covenant of Further Assurances

The *covenant of further assurances* is an undertaking in the form of a covenant in which the seller agrees to "...do such further acts for the purpose of perfecting the purchaser's title as the latter may reasonably require." (*Black's Law Dictionary, 5th Edition.*)

DELIVERY

A *deed* will only pass title when it is delivered. Delivery occurs when the grantor manifests an intent to complete delivery. Although there is no ritualistic physical act, the handing over of the deed to the grantee is generally good evidence that a delivery was intended.

The grantor cannot grant a future delivery to a grantee but can convey a future interest. For example, Frank hands a deed over to Trudy, saying, "I give you an interest in my property to take effect a year from today." This delivery would be valid. On the other hand, if the deed purported to convey a fee simple rather than a future interest, it would be an invalid delivery, and title would not pass.

A grantor may deliver a deed for a future or conditional delivery by use of an *escrow*. *Escrow* is "a system of documents given to a third person to hold until all conditions in a contract are fulfilled..." (*Black's Law Dictionary, 5th Edition.*)

Once a deed is delivered, the title passes to the grantee. An undelivered deed passes no title whatsoever, even if it has been recorded.

HELPFUL HINT #9

DEFINITIONS

1. **MARKETABLE TITLE**: Property which is free of encumbrances and reasonable doubt as to its validity.

2. **RISK PROVISIONS**: The allocation of income and expenses during the contract period, the risk of physical destruction before the settlement, the kind of payment required, and remedies for breach of the contract.

3. **CHAIN OF TITLE**: Consecutive conveyances affecting a specific parcel of land from the government or original source of title to the present holder.

HELPFUL HINT #10

REMEMBER

1. **Zoning** and subdivision restrictions often affect the marketability of title.
2. Generally, **physical defects** to the property do not affect marketability of title.
3. **Equitable conversion** affects title, not possession.
4. Before a contract is executed, all **risk of loss** from destruction of the property not caused by any party is upon the seller.
5. If the seller fails or refuses to convey the property at closing, the buyer can **withdraw** from the contract, seek specific performance, or sue for damages.

HELPFUL HINT #11

QUIZ

1. A________ is the usual **instrument** for conveying property.
2. Any **transfer in the interest** in land must be ________ and requires the identification of the ________.
3. ________________ are the **boundary lines** of land.
4. Name the three types of **deeds**.

Answers

1. Deed.
2. In writing, Grantee.
3. Metes and bounds.
4. Quitclaim, statutory, and warranty.

THE RECORDING SYSTEM

In General

The focus of this chapter will be on the claims of competing grantees for the same title. Generally, a *deed* only has to be delivered in order for it to pass title to the grantee.

Conversely, recordation cannot validate an undelivered deed. If a deed has been recorded, there is a presumption that it has been delivered. However, this presumption is rebuttable.

At common law, the system of priorities was *first in time, first in right*. This meant that if the grantor had conveyed his land twice, the first grantee to record the deed held title. The one exception to this rule was described in the *bona fide purchaser* principle.

Basically, a *bona fide purchaser* is "one who has purchased property for value without any notice of any defect in the title of the seller." (*Black's Law Dictionary, 5th Edition*.)

The reason for the preference of the *bona fide purchaser* principle over the *first in time* rule is based on the role of title searches in conveyancing. To make searches reliable, recording systems were developed. Recording systems made it necessary for anyone who acquired land to make it public so others could discover it and conversely penalize the person who failed to do so by permitting others to take priority.

Recording Systems

Every state has a recording system. A recording system consists of official records and various indexes affecting every piece of land in a county. Any instrument affecting title can be recorded. This includes easements, deeds, covenants, mortgages, and contracts for the sale of land

Grantor-Grantee and Grantee-Grantor Indexes

Most states have an index which references each of these documents. The most common index is the *Grantor-Grantee and Grantee-Grantor Indexes*. These types of indexes organize documents in alphabetical order according to the names of the parties.

Tract Index

Another type of index is the *Tract Index*. This index classifies documents according to the parcel they describe.

Recording Acts

There are three major recording acts which are primarily used in establishing the priority of persons claiming priority over land.

Notice Act

The first recording act is a *notice act*. This statute declares that an unrecorded instrument is void against any person who later takes an interest in the same property without notice of that instrument.

Notice-Race Act

The second recording act is called the *notice-race act.* It essentially states that ". . . the first grantee or mortgagee tc record in the chain of title without actual notice of a prior unrecorded deed or mortgage prevails." (*Black's Law Dictionary, 5th Edition.*) This act protects any subsequent purchaser who takes without notice and records first.

Race Act

The third recording act is the *race act*. This statute states that ". . . the party who records an instrument of conveyance has the better claim regardless of notice or prior unrecorded instruments." (*Black's Law Dictionary, 5th Edition.*) This type of statute hardly exists today because of its perceived unfairness.

Purchase for Value

To obtain the protection of a recording act, it is necessary for the subsequent purchaser to have given *value* for his instrument. If there was no value involved, the reliance was not detrimental and no great loss was incurred.

Examples of transactions which constitute payment of value are: payment of the purchase price, a mortgage to secure a prior debt, or partial payment.

Where value has not been paid, for example, where one takes by gift, there is no protection against prior unrecorded instruments.

Notice

As stated above, a subsequent purchaser prevails over a prior unrecorded instrument if he or she is without notice. He or she will not prevail if he or she had knowledge or should have known of the prior claim. There are three major types of notice: *actual knowledge, constructive notice,* and *inquiry notice.*

ACTUAL KNOWLEDGE

Actual knowledge is where the subsequent purchaser is actually aware of the prior claim. He or she generally will not prevail if he or she has *actual knowledge*.

Constructive Notice

Constructive notice is ". . . information or knowledge of a fact imputed by law to a person (although he may not actually have it), because he could have discovered the fact by proper diligence, and his situation was such as to cast upon him the duty of inquiring into it." (*Black's Law Dictionary, 5th Edition.*) Jurisdictions differ on what constitutes a diligent search.

Inquiry Notice

Inquiry notice refers to the duty imposed upon a purchaser to make a search of records and imputes to him or her such knowledge as a reasonable inquiry would produce. Courts apply this notice standard when the circumstances warranted an inquiry and that a reasonable search would have revealed the fact in question.

HELPFUL HINT #12

Discussion

1. Discuss the system of **priorities** for holding title to property.
2. Discuss the three major **recording acts** which are used in establishing priority over land.

MORTGAGES

IN GENERAL

A *mortgage* is another means of conveying property. It is "...an interest in land created by a written instrument providing security for the performance of a duty or the payment of a debt." (*Black's Law Dictionary, 5th Edition*).

A *mortgage* involves two documents. The first document essentially memorializes the basic obligation (usually a debt to pay). The second document is the *mortgage* which basically states that the *mortgagee*, or the one taking the *mortgage*, may reach the property of the person signing the document, referred to as the *mortgagor,* if the obligation (payment) is not made.

FORECLOSURE

If the *mortgagor* does not fulfill his or her obligation, the *mortgagee* can obtain relief by way of *foreclosure*. A *foreclosure* is "a termination of all rights of the mortgagor or his grantee in the property covered by the mortgage." (*Black's Law Dictionary, 5th Edition.*)

If a *mortgagor* fails to pay the debt within a certain period of time, the property can be sold at a public auction, rather than go automatically to the *mortgagee*. The proceeds from this sale are used to discharge the indebtedness.

Transfer of Interest

A *mortgagor* and a *mortgagee* may transfer their interest in the property. A *mortgagor* can convey her property, although the existence of the *mortgage* may mean that his or her title is not marketable unless it is paid off. The grantee of such property is not personally liable for any deficiency judgment unless he or she actually assumed the mortgage obligation.

A *mortgagee* can transfer the mortgage whether that document is physically handed over or not. The note also may be negotiable, allowing the transferee to take free of many defenses the *mortgagor* might otherwise have.

HELPFUL HINT #13

DEFINITIONS

1. **MORTGAGE**: A way to convey property by a written agreement securing performance of a duty or payment of a debt.

2. **FORECLOSURE**: A termination of all rights of the mortgagor or his or her grantee in the mortgaged property.

LAND RIGHTS

IN GENERAL

There are a variety of land rights which are affected by water and airspace, nuisance and trespass laws, fixtures and waste. This chapter will focus on those rights. It will also examine the standards which describe these rights.

WATER RIGHTS

A person's water rights depend upon whether the water flows *in a stream, over the surface of land, or is underground.*

Stream Water

There are basically three rights in stream water: *riparian rights, absolute rights*, and *correlative rights.*

Riparian Rights

Riparian rights refer to land which is adjacent to a stream. At common law, nonriparian owners did not have the right to take water from a stream when it would affect the rights of the *riparian* owners.

Absolute Right

A person who owned land which was adjacent to a stream or lake had an *absolute right* to take water under two conditions. The first was where removal of the water did not affect the quantity and quality of the flow of the stream. The second was where the water was removed for domestic uses on the riparian land, such as drinking and bathing.

Correlative Rights

Correlative rights "refers to doctrine which is applied to owners of land and their rights to use of their land with respect to rights of adjoining or lower riparian landowners in water or oil." *(Black's Law Dictionary, 5th*

Edition.) There are three different doctrines which regulate the rights of a *riparian* to draw water from a stream for nondomestic uses when the flow is affected.

Natural Flow Doctrine

The first doctrine is known as the *natural flow doctrine.* This doctrine states that every downstream *riparian* owner has an absolute right to have the stream come to him or her without alteration. Any alteration of the flow entitles him or her to enjoin an upstream for nondomestic use. This is the minority position among most jurisdictions.

Reasonable Use Doctrine

The second doctrine is the *reasonable use doctrine.* The rights of a downstream owner are governed by principles of reasonableness. These rights are weighed against the needs and intended uses of both the upstream and downstream users.

Prior Appropriation System

The third doctrine is the *prior appropriation system.* This system has mostly been used by arid western states. Under this system, the rights to take water are acquired by permit. Priority of use when water is scarce depends upon the date of the permit application. Nonriparians may obtain permits to take water which may be granted on certain conditions of use.

Surface Water

Surface water also includes certain rights. Generally, landowners are more concerned with disposing of surface waters rather than with capturing it. The major rules of surface water deal with the rights to get the water off their land.

Common Enemy Rule

About half the jurisdictions allow each owner to channel these waters away under the *common enemy rule.* Some courts subject this rule to a reasonable interference doctrine, requiring the owners to use reasonable techniques.

Civil Law Rule

The other jurisdictions follow the *civil law rule*. Under this rule, the owner of the lower land is prohibited from obstructing the natural flow of the water from the upper land. At the same time, the upper owner is prohibited from altering the natural drainage over the lower land.

Underground Water

Underground water usually deals with water which percolates through the soil and is sought by the overlying owners. The major rules here deal with their rights to drill and pump the water out.

Eastern Rule

The *Eastern rule* holds that the underground water is owned by the overlying owner. No overlying owner can complain as to the activities of another common overlying owner. This rule is generally applied where water is plentiful.

Western Rule

The *Western rule* is used in arid states. It limits the activities of overlying owners by applying a principle of reasonable use.

Trespass and Nuisance

A person who owns or possesses land is entitled to freedom from interference by others. There are two types of interference with property: *trespass* and *nuisance*.

Trespass

A *trespass* is "an unlawful interference with one's person, property, or rights." (*Black's Law Dictionary, 5th Edition*.) Fault and motive do not have to be proven in *trespass*.

Trespass is not limited to intrusion on land. It may occur overhead with, for example, a telephone wire or an airplane.

An owner or possessor may collect damages without proof of harm. If the *trespass* is continuing, there may be repeated recoveries. However, if no harm has occurred as result of the *trespass*, the damages will only be nominal. A court may order injunctive relief if there is a likelihood of the *trespass or where harm may be irreparable.*

Nuisance

Nuisance is ". . . that activity which arises from unreasonable, unwarranted or unlawful use by a person of his own property, working obstruction or injury to right of another, or to the public, and producing such material annoyance, inconvenience and discomfort that the law will presume resulting damage." (*Black's Law Dictionary, 5th Edition.*)

Unlike *trespass, nuisance* does not require a physical intrusion. However, *nuisance* does require harm. If the interference with a neighbor's use and enjoyment is regarded as unreasonable, the activity will be considered a *nuisance*. The unreasonable interference standard requires the court to balance the situations of the parties.

Airspace Rights

As mentioned earlier, rights in land are not limited to the surface. At common law, an owner was said to own "the heavens above."

Generally, landowners can develop their property as high as they please. The loss of light or view caused by a high-rise building is not actionable unless the neighbors have acquired special rights in that regard.

There are certain considerations which apply to invasions of airspace. For example, flights at high levels are not trespassory because airlanes have become public highways. However, flights below a permissible level may be considered trespassory.

Flights overhead may also be considered a *nuisance*. Often, an airport will acquire a large piece of land surrounding the airport to avoid liability for noise which jets create. Public policy denies injunctive relief to neighbors in such situations, limiting them to damages.

Fixtures

A person can also have rights in *fixtures* which relate to the land. A *fixture* is "an article in the nature of personal property which has been so annexed to the realty that it is regarded as part of the land." (*Black's Law Dictionary, 5th Edition.*)

Personalty becomes realty when three criteria are met. First, there has to be an intent to make the personalty, or *chattel*, a permanent part of the land. Second, if the *chattel* is actually affixed to the land, for example bathroom fixtures to a house, then the personalty becomes realty. Finally, there is a conversion from personalty to realty if the *chattel* has been specially adapted for the use of the land.

Where both the *chattel* and the land are owned by one owner, the sale of the real property transfers title to all of the fixtures as well. The consequences can be different when the *chattel* is owned by someone other than the owner of the realty. For example, when a tenant affixes a *chattel* to the land, it becomes a part of the realty. However, the law permits a tenant to remove *chattels* installed for the purposes of trade, even if they have become fixtures.

WASTE

Another right to land has to do with the use of the land. A person who possesses land is prohibited from using the land to cause *unreasonable injury* to the other holders in the same property. This is referred to as *waste.*

The standard test for *waste* is whether the act *substantially diminishes* the value of the other estate. The court balances the interests of both parties.

There are three main types of *waste: ameliorating waste, voluntary waste,* and *permissive waste.*

Ameliorating Waste

Ameliorating waste constitutes "a change in the physical characteristics of property by an unauthorized act of the tenant but which adds value and improves the property." (*Black's Law Dictionary, 5th Edition.*)

Voluntary Waste

Voluntary waste is also known as *active* or *positive waste*. It is the "....willful destruction or carrying away of something attached to the freehold..." (*Black's Law Dictionary, 5th Edition*.) For example, removing floors or shelves, or other things affixed to the freehold, is *voluntary waste*.

Permissive Waste

Permissive waste is "that kind of waste which is a matter of omission only...." (*Black's Law Dictionary, 5th Edition*.) Allowing a house to fall into disrepair is an example of *permissive waste*.

HELPFUL HINT #14

REMEMBER

1. There are three rights in **stream water**: riparian; absolute; and correlative.
2. The **natural flow doctrine** states that every downstream riparian owner has an absolute right to have the stream come to him or her without alteration.
3. The **Eastern rule** holds that underground water is owned by the overlying owner.
4. The **Western rule** limits activities of an overlying owner by applying a principal of reasonable use.
5. There are three main types of **waste**: ameliorating, voluntary, and permissive.

LAND REGULATION

IN GENERAL

Land use is subject to local, state, and regional regulations. The federal government does not directly influence land regulation, except on land that it owns. Some jurisdictions allow land-use regulations to be enacted by voter initiative. Voter regulation will depend on whether the regulation issue affects all residents.

LAND REGULATING BY PLANNING

There are a few basic forms of land-use regulation. The first is in the form of *planning*. Many states require that planning precede any land-use regulation, and thus create local planning boards. There is no settled definition of "planning," but land development must be in accord with a comprehensive plan.

Land Regulation by Zoning Laws

Zoning laws are another form of land-use regulation. *Zoning* is prescribed by ordinances and specify regulations regarding the zone characteristic of each parcel of land within a community. Some common types of use districts are residential, commercial, and agricultural.

Zoning laws can also set requirements regarding land coverage. For example, there may be a setback requirement where every building must be set back so many feet from the lot line. Further, they also may require that a building which occupies a certain size lot preserve a certain amount of open space.

Land Regulation Through Subdivision

A third type of land-use regulation is through *subdivision regulation*. When land is subdivided, a map of the subdivision must be recorded and approved. Subdivision regulation is different from zoning in that approval of a subdivision is more of a bargaining process between the subdivider and the planning department.

How are land-use regulations reviewed? Generally, the review is heard by property owners who object to the regulations or who oppose the lifting of a restriction. The regulation or restriction is presumed to be valid if it bears a rational relationship to a state objective.

Limitations to Land-Use Regulations

Land-use regulations will be held invalid on a number of grounds. The regulation must be fair in its enactment. That is, notice must be given. Also, Federal and state constitutions provide that private property cannot be taken without just compensation.

Judicial Relief

What kind of judicial relief is afforded if a land-use regulation is found invalid? In some cases, the community affected by the regulation may be given an opportunity to present a corrected regulation. The majority of courts are reluctant to grant damages, preferring to limit relief to invalidation of the regulation.

HELPFUL HINT #15

QUIZ

1. Land use is subject to __________, _________, and __________________ regulations.
2. What is prescribed by ordinance and specific regulations regarding the characteristic of each parcel of land within a community?
3. When land is subdivided, what must be recorded?

ANSWERS

1. Local, state, and regional.
2. Zoning.
3. A map.

CONCLUSION

Many of our current legal principles of real property come from English common law. Principles of real property have come to involve not only land rights, but water rights and the rights of airspace. When examining a real-property question, isolate the issue or issues by determining the type of interest involved, is it a present or future estate? How is the land held, for example, in adverse possession, concurrent ownership, as landlord-tenant? Some questions involve specific issues of possession and use, such as easements and covenants running with the land. Questions regarding a conveyance should alert you to issues of a valid contract, marketable title, performance, breach and damages, and delivery. You should be able to answer a real-property question successfully if you can identify the position of the parties and their corresponding rights.

BLACK-LETTER LAW SUMMARIES AND IMPORTANT TERMS

Possession

Adverse Possession: A method for the acquisition of property which, to be valid, must satisfy four elements: actual entry and possession of the land; open and notorious possession; continuous possession; and adverse to the owner's interest.

Freehold Estates

Estate: In property law, which derived from English common law and land law, the term estate is an interest in land which is or will be possessory and is measured in terms of duration.

Seisin: The term seisin is a "feudal" concept which is used to mean that a person has possession of land under a claim of freehold. Therefore, if one has possession and a freehold estate, they are said to "have seisin" of the land.

Fee Simple or Fee Simple Absolute: "O to A and his heirs."

Fee Tail: "O to A and the heirs of his body."

Life Estate: "O to A for life."

Life Estate Pur Autre Vie: "O to A for the life of B." A's estate is measured by the life of another.

Fee Simple Determinable: "O to A so long as no liquor is sold on the premises."

Fee Simple Subject to a Condition Subsequent: "O to A but if any liquor is ever sold on the premises, then O may re-enter the premises and terminate the estate."

Future Interests

Note: There are five kinds of estates which are referred to as future interests since they exist but are not possessory.

Possibility of Reverter: This future interest is only in the grantor and is always associated with a fee simple determinable.

Power of Termination or Right of Re-entry: This future interest is only in the grantor and is always associated with a fee simple subject to a condition subsequent.

Reversion: This future interest is only in the grantor and is associated with a life estate or an estate which is less than a fee simple.

<u>Remainder</u>: This future interest is only in a third person (never in the grantor) and takes effect upon the termination of a previous estate. "O to A for life and the remainder to Band his heirs."

Note: There are two main types of remainder: vested and contingent. Contingent remainders are subject to the rule against perpetuities but vested remainders are not.

<u>The Executory Interest</u>: This future interest is only in a third person (never in the grantor) and takes effect by cutting short a prior estate. There are two main types: shifting executory interests and springing executory interests.

<u>Rule in Shelley's Case</u>: "If a will or conveyance creates a freehold in A and purports to create a remainder in A's heirs or in the heirs of his body, the remainder will be deemed a fee simple or a fee tail."

Doctrine of Worthier Title: Under this doctrine "one cannot, by will or conveyance, give a remainder to his own heirs."

The Rule Against Perpetuities: The rule states that "no interest is good unless it must vest, if at all, not later than 21 years after some life in being at the creation of the interest."

Nonfreehold Estates

Note: There are four kinds of estates which are referred to as non-freehold estates since seisin does not attach to them.

Estate for Years: An estate for years is a lease with a definite term for a fixed period of time, such as a lease for five years.

Periodic Estate: A periodic estate is a lease, such as a month-to-month tenancy, which continues from one period to the next automatically.

Tenancy at Will: A tenancy at will has no stated duration and may be terminated at any time with notice to the other party.

Tenancy at Sufferance: If a tenant holds over at the end of a lease term, the hold-over period is referred to as a tenancy at sufferance.

Marital Estates

Dower: Under common law, the concept of dower allowed a widow to share in her husband's estate. The widow was entitled to one-third of any land in which the husband was seised during the term of their marriage.

Curtesy: Under common law, a widower was entitled to a life estate in any real property in which the wife had a freehold interest during the term of their marriage.

Tenancy by the Entirety: A special form of ownership for a husband and wife.

Tenancy by Community Property: A special form of ownership for a husband and wife in community property states, such as California and Arizona.

Concurrent Ownership

Joint Tenancy: A joint tenancy is a form of ownership where each tenant owns a whole interest. A joint tenancy will exist only if, under common law, the four unities of interest, title, time, and possession exist. There is a right to survivorship.

Tenancy in Common: In a tenancy in common, each tenant has a separate, divided interest. There is no right to survivorship.

Easements

Easement: An easement is a right or privilege to use the land of another. An easement may be affirmative (allows one to do a physical act on the land) or negative (prevents one from doing a physical act on the land).

Easement Appurtenant: An easement appurtenant benefits the holder in the use of a piece of land.

Dominant Tenement: The land for whose benefit the appurtenant easement is created.

Servient Tenement: The land that is burdened, or used, by the easement appurtenant is called the servient tenement.

Easement in gross: The benefit is not associated with a particular piece of land but rather is personal to the holder.

Profit or Profit a Prendre: The right to go onto the land of another to remove soil or a product of the soil. A profit would include the right to drill for oil, mine for minerals, or hunt and fish.

Covenants Running With the Land

Covenant: A covenant is a promise or a contract which may "run with the land" in that it will effect a subsequent purchaser of the land because the covenant remains with the land, not the owner.

Recording Statutes

Note: There are three types of recording acts.

Pure Race Statutes: The first to record a deed wins whether or not there is notice of other purchasers.

Pure Notice Statute: The emphasis is not on recordation but on notice. If a prior purchaser does not record a deed and a subsequent purchaser records first, the subsequent purchaser will not win if the subsequent purchaser did not have notice.

Race-Notice Statute: A subsequent purchaser is protected if he or she records first and has no actual notice of the earlier conveyance.

Water Rights

Diffused Surface Waters: These are waters which are spread over the surface of the ground with no recognizable channels or predicatable flow. The main question in connection with surface waters is the owner's right to drain the waters from his or her land.

Common Enemy Rule: Allows a property owner to dam, deflect, or move diffused surface waters.

Civil Law Doctrine: An owner may not channel or change the natural flow of diffused surface waters.

Reasonable Use Doctrine: An owner may make reasonable changes in the natural drainage of diffused surface waters.

Water in Watercourses (such as streams and lakes): The issue in this area is the right to appropriate water from watercourses. There are two conflicting theories: the common-law riparian rights theory and the statutory prior appropriation theory.

The Common Law Riparian Rights Theory: Under this theory, there is no advantage to an owner because of an established prior use. A riparian owner is one whose land abuts the stream or lake.

Prior Appropriation Doctrine: Water may be appropriated by a non-riparian owner and owners may have a priority use if they can establish prior appropriation of the waters.

Groundwater: Groundwater is water below the surface. Under the English Rule, an owner may draw all the water he can to the surface of his own land. Under the American "reasonable use rule", an owner may only draw a reasonable use of groundwater from under his property.

IMPORTANT CASES: ISSUES AND HOLDINGS

Adverse Possession

Ewing v. Burnet, 36 U.S. 41 (1837): The issue is whether the defendant who paid taxes on property, controlled entry onto the land, and brings trespass actions can claim title to the land under the theory of adverse possession. The court held that the defendant's acts were public, open, and notorious.

Freehold Estates

Cole v. Steinlauf, 136 A.2d 744 (1957): The issue is whether a conveyance to the defendant "and his assigns forever" provided the plaintiff with marketable title. The court held that since the action was not between the grantor and the defendant, in which such language could be construed as granting a fee simple absolute, the plaintiff could not be certain that the title was marketable.

Lewis v. Searles, 452 S.W. 2d 153 (1970): The issue is whether the plaintiff has a fee simple determinable from a grant which provided "to my niece so long as she remains single and unmarried. In the event that she marries, then the property shall be divided equally as follows..." The court found that the language of the grant did create a fee simple determinable rather than a life estate.

Concurrent Ownership

Jackson v. O'Connell, 177 N.E. 2d 194 (1961): The issue is whether an original grant to three sisters in which one of the sisters conveyed her interest to the second sister who died and bequeathed her interest to her four nieces severs the joint tenancy and creates a one-sixth interest in each one of the nieces. The court held that the conveyance between the sisters did sever the joint tenancy but only in connection with that share, and, therefore, the nieces had a one-twelth interest each which they held as tenants in common with the remaining sister (the original grantee).

Landlord-Tenant

Arbenz v. Exley, Watkins & Co., 50 S.E. 813 (1905): The issue in this case is whether a notice of vacating of premises was sufficient to constitute a notice to terminate. The court held that since the lease was for a period of one year, a written notice with a termination date was required and a notice to abandon was insufficient.

Easements

Finn v. Williams, 33 N.E. 2d 226 (1941): The issue in this case is whether an easement was created by necessity when the only route of access to a public highway was by a private road. The court held that an easement by necessity was created in that for the last forty years there was only one way to the public highway and that was over the private road. When the private road was closed by a subsequent purchaser of the parcel, the plaintiff acquired a right of way.

<u>Marantha Settlement Assn. v. Evans,</u> 122 A.2d 679 (1956): The issue is whether a grant in a deed in a developer's subdivision which granted to the grantee and his immediate family the right to use the subdivision's swimming pool is an easement appurtenant or an easement in gross. The court found that it was an easement appurtenant since it was intended to benefit purchasers in the subdivision as a whole.

Covenants Running With Land

<u>Wheeler v. Schad,</u> 7 Nev. 213 (1872): The issue is whether a promise to pay for the construction and repair of a dam made after a conveyance of a part of a mill site constituted a covenant running with the land. The court held that since there was no privity of estate, the burden did not run with the land when it was conveyed.

Tulk v. Moxhay, 41 Eng. Rep. 1143 (1848): The issue is whether an equitable remedy could be provided when there was no remedy at law since there was no horizontal privity between the parties. The court granted equitable relief for a covenant that was not enforceable at law.

Zoning and Land-Use Controls

Pennsylvania Coal Co. v. Mahon, 260 U.S. 393 (1922): The issue in this U.S. Supreme Court case is whether a Pennsylvania statute which forbade the mining of coal where the effects would cause a house to sink so impaired the right to mine coal that it was the equivalent of a taking. The court held, in the majority opinion, that the regulation was a taking and the state would have to compensate the coal company. The dissent by Justice Brandeis held that the regulation did not constitute a taking but merely the prohibition of a "noxious" use.

Note: The majority decision in this case has been practically invalidated by **Keystone Bituminous Coal Ass'n v. DeBenedictis**, 480 U.S. 470 (1987).

Note: Many of the zoning cases focus on constitutional issues and will not be addressed in this book.

Mortgages and Deeds

King v. Wegner, 549 P. 2d 986 (1976): The issue is whether a contract for the sale of land exists when there is no formal evidence of the sale. The court found that the parties were not bound without a written agreement.

Murphy v. Financial Development Corp., 495 A.2d 1245 (1985): The issue is whether a mortgagee owes a duty of good faith and a duty of diligence to a mortgagor. The court held that defendants did not exercise due diligence in refusing to set a minimum bid or seeking additional purchasers.

Recording Statutes

Patterson v. Bryant, 5 S.E. 2d 849 (1939): The issue is whether a recording statute will prevent the plaintiff from recovering for double dealing when the defendant transferred the same property to two different people. Under the recording statute, the second transferee took precedence over the first transferee since the first transferee recorded first. The court held the recording statute did not affect the plaintiff's right to recover damages.

Guerin v. Sunburst Oil & Gas Co., 218 P. 949 (1923): The issue is whether a bona fide purchaser for value has a duty to inquire about a reference in a chain of title. The court found that there is a duty of inquiry and since the plaintiff did not inquire, the plaintiff could not take the property free of an unrecorded lease.

WATER RIGHTS

Evans v. Merriweather, 4 Ill. 492 (1842): The issue is whether the construction of a dam which diverted all the water to one mill was an artificial or natural use and whether it was a reasonable use. The court found that since it was an artifical use, there was no entitlement to use all of the water.

APPROACHING EXAMINATION QUESTIONS

The practice questions are different from what you will see on a law-school exam. The questions in this book are simplified to allow you to gain practice and experience in identifying issues and integrating black-letter rules of law with material facts to create well-reasoned, logical analysis.

In approaching any examination question, whether it is a three-page, complex, multi-issue examination question or a simple paragraph, single-issue fact pattern, the principles for success are the same. There are many ways to write an examination question answer. The important point is to remember that you are writing a law-school examination and not a bar examination. Bar examiners are not reading your answer, but rather law professors who are reading your answer to determine if you know the law and if you have reasoned through the question to your conclusion.

It is not the conclusion which is of first importance on law-school examinations but rather the analysis. It is common for law students to reach a conclusion after reading the fact pattern and then generate the analysis rather than identifying the issues, material facts, and rules of law, and then writing analysis (reasoning) which leads to a conclusion.

The first step in writing any law-school examination is to identify the "call of the question." The "call of the question" is the question you are asked to answer. For example, "What are Jamie's rights?", "Is there an easement," "Who has the right to the groundwater?" The "call of the question" may be narrow or it may be broad. Law students are often tempted to write all that they know in response to a law-school examination when the "call of the question" may ask for limited information. Most law professors will not give extra points because you have extra information in your answer. They are looking to see if you have responded to the question asked with well-reasoned analysis. It is wise to avoid the temptation to write everything you have memorized if it is not applicable to the question before you.

If possible, try to familiarize yourself with the type of examinations your law professor writes and the answers he or she considers excellent. Each law professor may have a different style and preferred method for writing examination answers. There are some general tips which will assist you in the event your law professor has no sample examinations/answers or does not provide assistance in this area.

First, read the fact pattern carefully from beginning to end, making notes in the margin, highlighting important facts or words, and noting rules of law which you will need once you begin writing.

Second, identify the "call of the question." This will assist you in knowing what rules of law may be applicable and will enable you to focus your answer.

Third, you may want to write a brief outline on your scratch paper or devise an approach before you actually begin writing your examination answer.

Fourth, you may be familiar with the IRAC method. IRAC stands for issue, rule, analysis, conclusion. It is a method for generating your analysis. Although the IRAC method is useful, do not take the position that you must stand fast in that approach (unless so suggested by your law professor).

When writing your analysis, you want to progress in a logical and coherent manner, working your way through the question so that all material facts and rules of law are clearly intergrated in your response.

A suggested approach for writing your analysis in response to the "call of the question" is as follows:

1. Begin with a statement applicable to the "call of the question."

A. For example, if the "call of the question" is, "Does John have an easement across Peter's property?", then you might begin by stating, "In determining whether or not there is an easement, certain requirements must be satisfied. These requirements are..."

B. If the "call of the question" is, "What are Meagan's causes of action?," you might begin by stating, "Meagan might be able to prove adverse possession if she can establish..."

2. State the applicable rule of law. In example B above, you might write, "Adverse possession requires the open, notorious, and visible possession of the land of another for the statutory period." You might then state that a cause of action for adverse possession has four elements and then identify these elements.

3. Integrate the facts with the rules of law. You will now want to incorporate those facts which are material to illustrating the rule of law.

4. Generate reasoning by moving through the question in a logical and cohesive fashion by integrating the facts with the rules of law.

5. Reach a conclusion. At this stage it is appropriate to state a conclusion in response to the "call of the question." For example, "Based upon the facts, Meagan has a cause of action for adverse possession since she satisfied all of the necessary elements."

QUESTIONS

Question 1

Lance Landlord leases to Tippy Tenant for a term of two years at a monthly rent of $600. One year later, Tippy "subleases, transfers, and assigns" to Trent for "a period of one year from date." Thereafter, neither Tippy nor Trent pays rent to Lenny. What rights does Lenny have against Tippy? Against Trent?

QUESTION 2

Trooper Tenant rents an apartment in Luke Landlord's building. Access to his apartment is provided by a hallway also used by other tenants. Some of the tile in the hallway is warped and raised, and Trooper has asked Luke twice to either repair the raised tiles or warn tenants of the potential danger. Luke has not done so. Trooper trips and falls while walking down the hall. He sues Trooper for his resulting broken ankle. What is the outcome and why?

Question 3

Farmer Brown owns 200 acres which he uses for planting wheat. He also owns two acres about four miles away from the main 200 acres which he has not used in some time. Rick parks his camper on the land which is adjacent to this two acres and begins planting wheat on the two acres. He also begins paying taxes on the land. Rick continues planting and paying taxes for twenty years. Does this constitute adverse possession? Explain.

Question 4

Oliver Owner, owner of Whiteacre, orally agrees to sell Whiteacre to Barry for $30,000. Oliver executes a deed conveying Whiteacre to Barry and delivers the deed to Max, as escrow agent, telling Max to hand the deed to Barry when Barry brings in the $30,000. Before Barry arrives with the money, Oliver decides the price is too low and demands return of the deed from Max. Must Max return the deed?

QUESTION 5

Rex contracts to buy Omar Owner's vacant lot. At the time the contract is signed, the lot is zoned for residential use by the city council. Prior to closing, the city council amends the ordinance and the lot is zoned for commercial use exclusively. Can Rex rescind the contract?

Question 6

O.J. Owner conveys Greenacre to "Angela and her heirs so long as the premises are not used for the sale of beer, wine, or liquor, and if beer, wine, or liquor is sold on the premises, O.J. retains a right to re-enter the premises." Subsequently, Angela opens a restaurant on Greenacre which serves several dishes cooked with wine or flamed with brandy and at Sunday brunch offers a complementary glass of champagne. Angela's restaurant is successful, and ten years after its opening, Ben wants to buy it and add a bar. Please advise Ben.

QUESTION 7

On August 1, Lenny Landlord leases Whiteacre "to Tory Tenant for one year, beginning August 1." On the following September 30, Tory moves out without giving Lenny any notice. What are Lenny's rights?

Question 8

Loopy Landlord leases to Trixie Tenant for a term of three years at a monthly rent of $500; the lease provides that "Tenant hereby covenants to pay said rent in advance on the first of each month." The lease also states that "Tenant shall not sublet or assign without the permission of Landlord." Six months later, Trixie, with the permission of Loopy, transfers to Tory for the balance of the term. Thereafter, Tory pays the rent directly to Loopy for several months, then defaults. Loopy sues Trixie for the rent due. What is the outcome?

QUESTION 9

Torpedo Tenant and her husband lease a house from Lucky Landlord. One day while Torpedo is working in the backyard of the house, she is injured in a cave-in caused by a defective cesspool. Similar events had occurred earlier with two other tenants, but Lucky claims he had no knowledge of them. Torpedo also claims that Lucky did know of the earlier events. Torpedo sues for personal injuries. What is the result?

Question 10

For rent payments of $800 a month, Luther Landlord leases Whiteacre "to Timmy Tenant for the duration of the recession." What estate does Timmy have?

ANSWERS

ANSWER 1

A tenant has a leasehold interest. It is fully transferable unless stated otherwise in the lease. The two main forms of transfer are assignment and sublease. An assignment is a transfer to another of any lease of any right therein. The assignee (Trent) becomes the new tenant of the landlord. If a tenant who assigns is no longer in privity of estate, and the assignee Trent fails to pay his rent, she remains liable. Therefore, under an assignment, Trent failed to pay rent to Lance the landlord and Tippy is, therefore, responsible. Lance can sue Tippy for the rent if Trent fails to pay. Tippy can then bring suit against Trent for reimbursement. In order for Lance to enforce the assignment, there must be an executed release which terminates the liability between himself and Tippy. This is the only way Tippy can be released from further liability. A sublease is different from an assignment because the tenant who subleases is a landlord to his sublessee.

There is no privity between Lance, the original landlord and Trent, the sublessee. Therefore, neither can sue the other. If the sublessee fails to pay and the tenant fails to perform, the landlord can terminate the lease and the sublease. Lance's rights will depend on whether this was an assignment or sublease.

ANSWER 2

A common area, such as the hallway, is the responsibility of the landlord. He or she is liable for this area. The landlord is deemed to have possession of the common areas while the tenants only have use of these areas. Therefore, landlords have a duty to inspect, repair, and maintain common areas for their tenants. Tenants can recover from landlords if they show failure of due care. Here, Trooper told Luke, his landlord, twice to repair the raised and warped tiles. Because Luke had ample notice of the danger, Trooper can recover damages for his broken ankle.

Answer 3

Adverse possession is a way in which a person can hold land. Most states allow a person to take land adversely if they meet certain requirements, including a statutory period which may range from five to twenty years. There are four essential requirements to prove adverse possession: actual entry and possession of the land, open and notorious possession of the land, continuing possession, and adverse possession. The first requirement is met because Rick lives in his camper on the property and has farmed this land for 20 years. The second requirement also is met because Rick lives about four miles away from Farmer John, and he has openly planted his wheat. The continuous possession element is met because planting seasonally qualifies as a continuous act. The fourth requirement is met because his possession was uninterrupted. Because all of these elements have been satisfied, there is a valid adverse possession.

ANSWER 4

The issue here is whether a valid delivery has been made. Escrow agents are often used to protect both parties to a contract. Here, Oliver handed the deed to Max with the instructions to deliver the deed to Barry contingent upon the receipt of the $30,000. If the grantor retains control over the title or retains the right to revoke escrow, the escrow will be invalid, and no delivery will have occurred. Generally, most courts permit the grantee to who deposits a deed in escrow to revoke the escrow itself unless there is an enforceable contract between the buyer and seller. Oliver and Barry made an oral agreement for the sale of Greenacre. They failed to comply with the *Statute of Frauds* so there is no enforceable contract. Even though Oliver has given the deed to a third party with delivery instructions, the escrow will be invalid, and Oliver will be allowed to revoke the escrow and get back his deed.

ANSWER 5

A contract for the sale of real property must include an intent to be bound, legal consideration, a writing, time for performance, and risk provisions. If there is a writing, we must ask whether Rex intended that the property be used for residential purposes. If this was an illusory promise, a court may declare the contract is unenforceable because the terms have changed. If Rex was planning on using the property for residential use and the zoning laws changed prior to conveyance, there is a material alteration of the terms of the contract. Zoning and subdivision restrictions often do not affect marketability, but here the zoning laws changed prior to closing, which will allow Rex to rescind the contract.

ANSWER 6

Angela has a fee simple absolute subject to a condition subsequent. O.J. retains a right of re-entry. This right gives Oscar the ability to take back the estate if the condition subsequent (sale of beer, liquor, and wine) occurs. For O.J. to re-enter the property, he must take some action and terminate Angela's interest in the land. According to the facts, Angela has been serving complimentary glasses of champagne and selling entrees cooked in alcohol for ten years. O.J. has not made any attempt to retake possession. Essentially, the mere sale of alcohol will not terminate the estate. O.J. must file an action against Angela to retake possession. Estates conveyed with a condition subsequent have a relatively short statute of limitations. Here, O.J. has made no attempt to remove Angela from the property, so it is probably safe for Ben to build his bar. Yet, Ben needs to be advised that O.J. may still have the right to re-enter, if not barred by a statute of limitations, and terminate Ben's estate.

Answer 7

There are four categories of tenancies. The tenancy for years, which is also known as a tenancy for a term, is a tenancy for a fixed period of time. This type of tenancy is usually is writing. Lenny has no rights, unless they are expressly addressed in writing. The term can be extended or even shortened, but only by mutual agreement. So, when Tory stayed on the additional month and Lenny took the rent, an implied agreement was reached. Again, in the absence of a writing, Lenny has no rights. If a tenant remains in possession after the term of the tenancy has expired and continues to pay rent, a periodic tenancy may arise. A periodic tenancy is terminated when one party gives timely notice which must be at least one time period. In this case, it would appear that there may also be a tenancy at sufferance. Tory stayed over the expiration date, and Lenny has not yet taken any action. If Lenny took Tory's rent money for that month, then Lenny has no rights against Tory.

ANSWER 8

The issue is what rights the parties have after the assignment. After an assignment, the original tenant is bound to keep his promise regarding the leased premises. If he assigns his interest, his privity with the lessor still remains so the lessor may still sue if the promise is not kept. Tory's breach of the lease agreement has put Trixie in jeopardy of a lawsuit for the rent due plus damages.

ANSWER 9

A landlord can be held liable for injuries caused by latent defects if they were known to him and not disclosed to the tenant. In this case, however, Lucky Landlord says he was not aware of this problem. There are a number of code compliances (health and safety) which are imposed on landlords and property owners. At common law, a landlord was not responsible for defects on the premises. Subsequent defects were the responsibility of the tenant. A landlord's duty is disclosure of the danger and not repair. However, since there have been a number of cave-in events, the court will question whether the landlord should have been aware of them. In the event Lucky's ignorance regarding the cave-ins is legitimate, Torpedo Tenant would have a difficult time bringing a suit for personal injury since she herself was aware of the cave-ins.

Answer 10

There are four types of tenancies: a tenancy for years, periodic tenancy and tenancy at sufferance. A tenancy for years has a specific start and end date. Since the end of the recession cannot be reasonably determined, Timmy does not have a tenancy for years. A periodic tenancy is for a fixed period of time until the landlord gives notice of the termination. This does not seem to be the case here because the period that this lease runs is continual and automatically renewed unless proper and timely steps are taken to terminate. In our case, we know a specific act (the end of the recession) will end the lease. A tenancy at will lasts only as long as the landlord and tenant desire. There is no predetermined termination date. Each may terminate at any time. This lease will last until the war ends. Of all four, the most fitting would be the periodic tenancy.

MOCK MULTI-STATE EXAMINATION QUESTIONS

1. Grantor owns Greenacre in fee simple. Grantor executes and delivers a deed to Greenacre with the following granting clause:

"To Penelope and Paula for their joint lives and upon the death of the first of them to die to the survivor, but if Rachel outlives both of them, then to Rachel."

As a result of the grant, which of the following is the most accurate statement regarding the ownership rights of Greenacre?

1. Penelope and Paula are joint tenants in fee simple defeasible, and Rachel has executory interest.

continued on the next page

2. Penelope and Paula have a joint life estate for the life of the one who lives the longest, and Penelope, Paula and Rachel have contingent remainders.

3. Penelope and Paula are tenants in common for the life of the first of them to die, Penelope and Paula have contingent remainders in fee simple defeasible, and Rachel has an executionary interest.

4. There is no legal difference between the results reached in alternatives (A), (B), or (C).

2. Symphony was the simple fee owner of Whiteacre, a 10-acre tract located in southern California. When Symphony moved to Arizona, Cactus took possession of Whiteacre. Cactus' possession has, at all times, complied with the requirements of the applicable adverse possession statute in effect.

Twelve years after Cactus took possession, Symphony died without a will, with Mozart, his eight-year-old son, as his only surviving heir. Nine years after Symphony's death, when Mozart was seventeen, Bach, who was Mozart's guardian, discovered that Cactus was in possession of Whiteacre. In California, the statutory period of adverse possession is twenty years and the age of majority is eighteen.

Which of the following correctly describes the state of title to Whiteacre?

continued on the next page

1. Cactus has acquired title by adverse possession.

2. Cactus will not acquire title unless he continues in adverse possession for an additional one year, or until Mozart reaches the age of eighteen.

3. Cactus will not acquire title unless he continues in adverse possession for an additional eight years, making a total of twelve years after Symphony's death.

4. Cactus will not acquire title unless he continues in adverse possession for an additional ten years, or nine years after Mozarrt attains the age of eighteen.

3. Over the last several months, Douglas had been negotiating with Daniel to purchase Blackacre. On March 28, 1996, they entered into a contract which provided in part: "I, Daniel, agree to convey good and marketable title to Douglas thirty days from the date of this contract." The stated purchase price for Blackacre was $1.5 million.

On April 15, 1996, Douglas told Daniel that his title search indicated that Watson, not Daniel, was the owner of record of the property. Daniel told Douglas that he had been in adverse possession of Blackacre for twenty-five years. The statutory period of adverse possession in this jurisdiction is twenty years.

The next day, Douglas verified that Daniel had, in fact, been in adverse possession of Blackacre for twenty-five years. At the closing, Daniel tendered a deed, but Douglas refused to pay the purchase price or take possession of Blackacre because he claimed Daniel could not convey "good and marketable title."

continued on the next page

In an appropriate action by Daniel against Douglas for specific performance, the seller will:

1. Prevail, because he has "good and marketable title" by adverse possession.
2. Prevail, because Daniel's action for specific performance is an actio in rem to which Watson is not a necessary party.
3. Not prevail, because an adverse possessor takes title subject to an equitable lien from the dispossessed owner.
4. Not prevail, because Douglas cannot be required to buy a lawsuit even if the probability is great that Douglas would prevail against Daniel.

4. Sarah and Peter own Treetop as joint tenants. If Sarah transfers her interest by quitclaim deed to Suzanne, without Peter's knowledge, what interest, if any, does Suzanne have in Treetop?

1. No interest.
2. An undivided one-half interest with rights of survivorship.
3. An undivided one-half interest without right of survivorship.
4. A lien against the entire property.

5. Under the facts in Question 4, assume that Sarah and Peter are married and own Treetop as tenants by entirety. If Sarah transfers her interest in Treetop by quitclaim deed to Suzanne, without Peter's knowledge, what interest, if any, does Suzanne have?

1. No interest.
2. An undivided one-half interest with right of survivorship.
3. An undivided one-half interest without right of survivorship.
4. A lien against the entire property.

6. In 1990, Ralph Turnip executed a deed in which he conveyed Redacre for one dollar "to Rosebud for life, then to Tulip for life, but if Tulip moves to England, to Daffodil for the life of Tulip, then to the heirs of Tulip if Tulip does not move to England and to the heir of Daffodil if Tulip moves to England." This deed was promptly recorded.

During Ralph Turnip's lifetime, Tulip's interest may best be described as a:

1. Contingent remainder
2. Shifting executory interest
3. Vested remainder subject to complete divestiture
4. Vested remainder subject to partial divestiture

7. Based on the facts in Question 6, during Turnip's lifetime, Daffodil's interest may best be described as a:

1. Life estate pur autre vie.
2. Contingent remainder pur autre vie.
3. Vested remainder pur autre vie.
4. Shifting executory interest pur autre vie.

8. Based on the facts in Question 6, in 1993, Tulip moved to England. The interest of Daffodil's heirs in Redacre would be construed as a (an):

1. Indefeasibly vested remainder.
2. Contingent remainder.
3. Alternative remainder.
4. Shifting executory interest.

9. Richard, owner of Blueacre, granted to Molly, owner of Silveracre, an easement of way. Richard then went to live in Texas. Molly moved into possession of Blueacre and used it openly and exclusively, paying the taxes for 28 years. Molly did not use the easement during that time. Richard returned and tried to evict Molly from Blueacre. The court held that Molly had acquired Blueacre by adverse possession. Molly then sold Blueacre back to Richard who then put a chain across the easement. Molly has now brought an action to remove the chain.

In most jurisdictions, Molly will:

1. Lose because she abandoned the easement
2. Lose because she did not use the easement for the statutory period of 20 years
3. Lose because, rather than using the easement, he took posession of Blueacre.
4. Win because mere non-use of an easement does not extinguish it.

10. O, the fee simple owner of Whiteacre, devised it "to A and B as tenants in common." Thereafter, A died intestate, leaving daughter, D, as his only surviving heir. While A's estate was in administration, B agreed to convey his interest in Whiteacre to D.

Which of the following would be a valid conveyance by C:

1. To the estate of A and his successors and assigns
2. To the heirs and assigns of A
3. To D and her heirs and assigns
4. To A as a former tenant in common with remainder to D.

11. Jeremy's will devised Cowacre "to my friend Carla for her love and concern for my cows, but if my cow, Spitfire does not receive proper care, then to my daughter, Lilly and her heirs, if Lilly is alive, otherwise to the Cow Club of New Mexico."

Carla has a:

1. Fee simple determinable
2. Fee simple subject to condition subsequent
3. Fee simple subject to an executory interest
4. Contingent remainder

12. Under the facts in Question 11, the rule against perpetuities is enforced in this jurisdiction. Which statement(s) is (are) correct concerning Lilly's interest in Cowacre?

I. It is a contingent remainder

II. It is a shifting executory interest

III. It is void under the Rule Against Perpetuities

1. I and II
2. II only
3. I and III
4. II and III

MOCK MULTI-STATE EXAMINATION ANSWERS

ANSWER 1

Answer 2 is the most accurate. Penelope and Paula have a life estate for their joint lives. At the death of either of them, the life estate terminated. All the parties have a contingent remainder in fee simple.

ANSWER 2

Answer 1 is the most accurate. Cactus' adverse possession is past the twenty-year requirement.

Answer 3

Answer 4 is the most accurate. Title established by adverse possession is free from encumbrance. However, the buyer did not bargain for title which was acquired by adverse possession, which is not normally considered "marketable" title.

Answer 4

Answer 3 is the most accurate. When a joint tenant conveys his or her interest, it severs the joint tenancy and a tenancy in common is the result.

Answer 5

Answer 1 is the most accurate. In a tenancy by entirety, a party cannot convey his or her interest without the other party's consent.

Answer 6

Answer 3 is the most accurate. Tulip's interest is vested but is subject to complete divestiture.

Answer 7

Answer 4 is the most accurate. It is a shifting executory interest since it cuts short a prior estate, and it is for the life of another, so it is pur autre vie.

Answer 8

Answer 2 is the most accurate. It is a contingent remainder since the heirs are not ascertainable.

Answer 9

Answer 3 is the most accurate. Since the dominant and servient estates have merged, the easement is extinguished.

Answer 10

Answer 3 is the most accurate. This is a simple question of choosing the obvious answer.

Answer 11

Answer 3 is correct. Carla has a fee simple which is subject to Lilly's executory interest.

Answer 12

Answer 4 is the most accurate. Executory interests are subject to the Rule Against Perpetuities. Lilly's interest will not vest within Carla's lifetime.

INDEX TO CASES

INDEX

A-B-C

E-F

G-H-I-J-K-L

M-N-O-P

Q-R-S-T

U-V-W-X-Y-Z

CONTENTS

PREFACE

Understanding the characteristics and trends of the federal workforce is important because, among other things, agencies accomplish their missions via that workforce. Total personnel costs (direct compensation and benefits) for all federal employees (civilian and military, current employees and retirees) were estimated at more than $523 billion in 2008, and civilian personnel costs in the executive branch alone were estimated at about $194 billion. Three cabinet departments — the Departments of Defense (DOD), Veterans Affairs (DVA), and Homeland Security (DHS) — accounted for almost 60% of the nearly 1.9 million executive branch civilian employees in 2008. The duty stations for more than 35% of these employees were in four states (California, Virginia, Texas, and Maryland) and the District of Columbia, and DOD was the top federal employer in 35 states. DOD also employed more than 90% of federal civilian employees in foreign countries, and was the top federal employer in U.S. territories. The federal workforce grew by more than 120,000 employees between 2000 (the low point during the last 10 years) and 2008, with the growth concentrated in homeland security-related agencies and DVA. Civilian employment in other agencies (including DOD and most independent agencies) declined during the last 10 years.

Chapter 1-The number of blue-collar and clerical federal jobs declined between 1998 and 2008, but the number of professional and administrative jobs increased during this period. The percentage of the federal workforce that was made up of minorities also increased, but the percentage that was women remained almost constant. Although women and minorities represented an increasing portion of the growing professional and administrative groups, the representation of women and minorities in the Senior Executive Service was less than their presence in the overall workforce. The federal workforce was somewhat older in 2008 than it was in 1998, but the average length of service declined from 15.2 years in 1998 to 14.7 years in 2008.

The number of white-collar employees in the General Schedule (GS) pay system declined during the last 10 years, while the number of employees in agency-specific pay systems (primarily at DOD and DHS) increased dramatically (from less than 1% of the workforce in 1998 to 16% in 2008). If these trends continue, the GS system will cover less than half of the federal civilian workforce by the year 2020. The average salary of the workforce was $69,061 in 2008, but average salaries varied substantially between and within federal agencies and pay systems.

Although the federal workforce has grown somewhat in recent years, a 2006 study estimated that the "hidden" federal workforce of contractors and grantees grew by more than 50% between 1999 and 2005, when it reportedly included more than 10.5 million jobs in 2005. That figure is more than twice as large as the combined total of all three branches of government, the U.S. Postal Service, the intelligence agencies, the armed forces, and the Ready Reserve.

Chapter 2- The federal workforce, like the nation's workforce as a whole, is aging. As experienced employees retire, they leave behind critical gaps in leadership and institutional knowledge, increasing the challenges government agencies face in maintaining a skilled workforce. We and others have emphasized the need to hire and retain older workers as one part of a comprehensive strategy to address expected labor shortages. The Office of Personnel Management (OPM), as the government's central personnel management agency, is responsible for helping agencies manage their human capital.

Chapter 3- To address the challenges that the nation faces, it will be important for federal agencies to change their cultures and create the institutional capacity to become high-performing organizations. This includes recruiting and retaining a federal workforce able to create, sustain, and thrive in organizations that are flatter, results-oriented, and externally focused.

In: Federal Workforce Trends
Editor: Claude R. Lewis

ISBN 978-1-60692-830-1

Chapter 1

THE FEDERAL WORKFORCE: CHARACTERISTICS AND TRENDS*

Curtis W. Copeland

ABSTRACT

Understanding the characteristics and trends of the federal workforce is important because, among other things, agencies accomplish their missions via that workforce. Total personnel costs (direct compensation and benefits) for all federal employees (civilian and military, current employees and retirees) were estimated at more than $523 billion in 2008, and civilian personnel costs in the executive branch alone were estimated at about $194 billion. Three cabinet departments — the Departments of Defense (DOD), Veterans Affairs (DVA), and Homeland Security (DHS) — accounted for almost 60% of the nearly 1.9 million executive branch civilian employees in 2008. The duty stations for more than 35% of these employees were in four states (California, Virginia, Texas, and Maryland) and the District of Columbia, and DOD was the top federal employer in 35 states. DOD also employed more than 90% of federal civilian employees in foreign countries, and was the top federal employer in U.S. territories. The federal workforce grew by more than 120,000 employees between 2000 (the low point during the last 10 years) and 2008, with the growth concentrated in homeland

* This is an edited, excerpted and augmented edition of a Congressional Research Service publication RL34685, dated September 30, 2008.

security-related agencies and DVA. Civilian employment in other agencies (including DOD and most independent agencies) declined during the last 10 years.

The number of blue-collar and clerical federal jobs declined between 1998 and 2008, but the number of professional and administrative jobs increased during this period. The percentage of the federal workforce that was made up of minorities also increased, but the percentage that was women remained almost constant. Although women and minorities represented an increasing portion of the growing professional and administrative groups, the representation of women and minorities in the Senior Executive Service was less than their presence in the overall workforce. The federal workforce was somewhat older in 2008 than it was in 1998, but the average length of service declined from 15.2 years in 1998 to 14.7 years in 2008.

The number of white-collar employees in the General Schedule (GS) pay system declined during the last 10 years, while the number of employees in agency-specific pay systems (primarily at DOD and DHS) increased dramatically (from less than 1% of the workforce in 1998 to 16% in 2008). If these trends continue, the GS system will cover less than half of the federal civilian workforce by the year 2020. The average salary of the workforce was $69,061 in 2008, but average salaries varied substantially between and within federal agencies and pay systems.

Although the federal workforce has grown somewhat in recent years, a 2006 study estimated that the "hidden" federal workforce of contractors and grantees grew by more than 50% between 1999 and 2005, when it reportedly included more than 10.5 million jobs in 2005. That figure is more than twice as large as the combined total of all three branches of government, the U.S. Postal Service, the intelligence agencies, the armed forces, and the Ready Reserve.

INTRODUCTION

The work of the federal government is done via its workforce, so understanding the characteristics and trends of that workforce is a critical part of understanding how the federal government can better accomplish its various missions. As the Government Accountability Office (GAO) said in May 2008,

> The importance of a top-notch federal workforce cannot be overstated. The nation is facing new and more complex challenges in the 21st century as various forces are reshaping the United States and its place in the world.... To address

> these challenges, it will be important for federal agencies to change their cultures and create the institutional capacity to become high-performing organizations. This includes recruiting and retaining employees able to create, sustain, and thrive in organizations that are flatter, results-oriented, and externally focused and that collaborate with other governmental entities as well as with the private and nonprofit sectors to achieve desired outcomes.[1]

In 2001, however, GAO identified the management of the federal workforce as a government-wide "high-risk" area because federal agencies lacked a strategic approach to workforce management that integrated those efforts with their missions and goals.[2]

Understanding the federal workforce is also important for a variety of other reasons. Personnel costs for both current and former employees represent a substantial portion of many agencies' budgets, and a significant portion of the total federal budget. Some federal agencies are major employers in certain states, and tens of thousands of federal employees work outside of the United States. The federal workforce is also expected by some to reflect the gender, racial, and ethnic diversity of the country as a whole. In addition, understanding recent changes in the overall size and composition of the federal workforce can indicate what changes may lie in the future.

COST AND SIZE OF THE FEDERAL WORKFORCE

Determining the size or cost of the federal workforce first requires a determination of what should be considered "the federal workforce," and what are considered relevant costs associated with that workforce. Federal budget documents distinguish federal personnel costs in terms of (1) direct compensation (e.g., salaries and bonuses) versus personnel benefits (e.g, health benefits and life insurance), (2) civilian employees versus military employees, and (3) current employees versus retired employees. The documents also show costs specific to the U.S. Postal Service and the Department of Defense (DOD), and separately show costs for the legislative and judicial branches of the federal government.

According to the FY2009 federal budget, and as shown in Table 1 below, total federal personnel costs (i.e., direct compensation and benefits) in 2008 for all groups (i.e., civilian and military, current employees, and retirees) were estimated at more than $523 billion. Direct compensation costs for current civilian employees (including all three branches of government and the U.S. Postal Service) were estimated at just under $190 billion. Civilian compensation costs for just the executive branch were estimated at nearly $144 billion, with DOD constituting about one-third of that total. In comparison, direct compensation costs for the legislative and judicial branches were relatively small (less than $5 billion combined). Compensation costs for employees of the U.S. Postal Service are almost entirely funded by postal fees, not appropriations. Some federal regulatory agencies (e.g., the Securities and Exchange Commission, the Nuclear Regulatory Commission, and the Federal Communications Commission) are also entirely or primarily funded through fees rather than appropriations.

According to the Office of Personnel Management (OPM), and as shown in Table 2 below, there were slightly more than 2.7 million employees in the total federal civilian workforce (all three branches plus the U.S. Postal Service) in September 2004 — down from nearly 3.0 million in September 1994.[3] From the beginning to the end of this period, the number of executive branch civilian employees declined by nearly 259,000 employees,[4] driven largely by reductions in the Department of Defense (DOD, down nearly 212,000 employees) and the U.S. Postal Service (down by more than 55,000).[5] The number of legislative branch employees declined somewhat during this period (down about 5,000 employees), while the number of judicial branch employees increased somewhat (up nearly 6,000).

Table 1. Estimated Civilian and Military Personnel Compensation and Benefits, 2008

(millions of dollars)

Organizational/ Employee Grouping	Cost		
	Direct Compensation	Personnel Benefits	Total Compensation
Civilian Personnel Costs			
Department of Defense (DOD)	$46,040	$12,367	$58,407
Executive Branch — Non-DOD	$97,604	$38,297	$135,901
Postal Service	$41,356	$18,609	$59,965
Legislative Branch	$1,988	$548	$2,536

Organizational/ Employee Grouping	Cost		
	Direct Compensation	Personnel Benefits	Total Compensation
Judicial Branch	$2,672	$879	$3,551
Total Civilian	$189,660	$70,700	$260,360
Military Personnel Costs			
DOD	$82,510	$48,608	$131,118
Other Uniformed Personnel	$2,717	$1,040	$3,757
Total Military	$85,227	$49,648	$134,875
Civilian and Military Personnel Costs	$274,887	$120,348	$395,235
Retiree Costs			
Civilian	$65,522	$8,872	$74,394
Military	$45,480	$8,349	$53,829
Total Retiree	$111,002	$17,221	$128,223
Grand Total — Civilian and Military, Active and Retiree	$385,889	$137,569	$523,458

Source: U.S. Office of Management and Budget, Budget of the U.S. Government: Analytical Perspectives; Fiscal Year 2009, Table 24-3.

Note: "Personnel benefits" for retirees includes health benefits and (for civilian personnel) life insurance.

Table 2. Trends in Federal Civilian Employment, 1994 – 2004

(in thousands)

	1994	1996	1998	2000	2002	2004
Legislative Branch	35.4	31.5	30.5	31.2	30.9	30.0
Judicial Branch	28.0	29.6	31.7	32.2	34.7	33.8
Executive Branch	2,908.2	2,786.3	2,727.3	2,644.8	2,649.9	2,649.3
DOD	879.9	795.9	717.9	676.3	670.2	668.2
Non-DOD	1,205.6	1,138.1	1,137.9	1,107.8	1,168.1	1,213.5
U.S. Postal Service	822.7	852.3	871.5	860.7	811.6	767.6
Total	2,971.6	2,847.4	2,789.5	2,708.1	2,715.5	2,713.2

Source: OPM's The Fact Book: 2005 Edition, p. 7.

These totals do not, however, include employees in the intelligence agencies, members of the active armed forces, or members of the reserve forces. The number of employees in the intelligence agencies is classified, but has been estimated at more than 100,000.[6] FY2009 appropriations legislation authorizes nearly 1.4 million members of the active armed forces,[7] and in September 2007, DOD reported that the "Ready Reserve" strength was more than 1 million.[8]

The OPM workforce data also do not include federal contractors and grantees. The exact number of direct and indirect federal contract and grant jobs is unknown, but Paul Light of New York University has estimated the total to be more than 10.5 million in 2005 — more than twice as many as the combined total of all three branches of government, the U.S. Postal Service, the intelligence agencies, the armed forces, and the Ready Reserve.[9] As Table 3 below shows, the estimated number of federal contract jobs increased by more than 70% between 1999 and 2005 (from more than 4.4 million to more than 7.6 million) — a change that was reportedly driven almost entirely by increased spending at DOD.[10] The table also shows that, taken together, the number of federal contract and grant jobs increased by more than 50% during this six-year period.

Table 3. Number of Direct and Indirect Federal Contract and Grant Jobs, 1999 and 2005

			Increase	
	1999	2005	Number	Percent
Federal contract jobs	4,441,000	7,634,000	3,193,000	71.9%
Federal grant jobs	2,527,000	2,892,000	365,000	14.4%
Total	6,968,000	10,526,000	3,558,000	51.1%

Source: Paul C. Light, The New True Size of Government, August 2006.

OPM's Central Personnel Data File (CPDF) is the most comprehensive, authoritative, and up-to-date database of federal executive branch employees, but it does not include information for certain executive branch agencies (e.g., the intelligence agencies) and certain entities that are sometimes considered part of the federal government (e.g., the U.S. Postal Service). It also does not include contractors, grantees, members of the armed forces, reservists, federal employees in the judicial branch, or most employees in the legislative branch.[11]

The data provided in the remainder of this report focus on civilian employees in executive branch departments and agencies. Unless otherwise noted, the data are drawn from OPM's "FedScope" website ([http://www.fedscope.opm.gov]), which is based on the CPDF. According to FedScope, in March 2008, there were 1,885,490 employees in the federal agencies that the CPDF covers.

Federal Civilian Employment by Agency

As Figure 1 and Table 4 below show, DOD was by far the largest federal agency in March 2008 (669,926 civilian employees), followed by the Department of Veterans Affairs (DVA, 263,667 employees) and the Department of Homeland Security (DHS, 170,663 employees). These three cabinet departments accounted for nearly 60% of the federal civilian workforce. More than 91% of federal civilian employees worked in one of the 15 cabinet departments. Among independent federal agencies (i.e., those agencies that are not part of a cabinet department), more than 65% of employees (108,701 of 166,845) were in four agencies: the Social Security Administration (SSA), the National Aeronautics and Space Administration (NASA), the Environmental Protection Agency (EPA), and the General Services Administration (GSA).

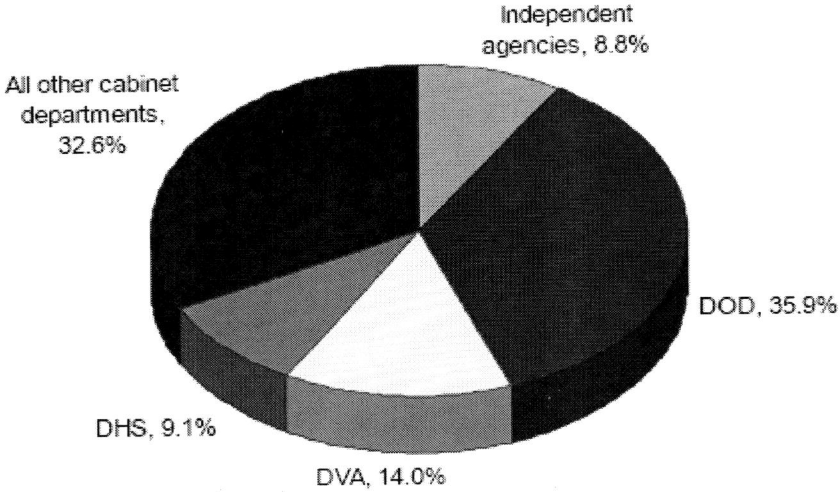

Source: OPM's FedScope database.

Figure 1. Federal Civilian Workforce, March 2008.

Table 4. Number of Federal Civilian Employees by Department and Major Independent Agency, March 2008

Department/Agency	Number of Civilian Employees
Cabinet Departments	
Department of Defense	669,926
Department of Veterans Affairs	263,667
Department of Homeland Security	170,663
Department of the Treasury	118,555
Department of Justice	106,635

Department/Agency	Number of Civilian Employees
Department of Agriculture	95,513
Department of Health and Human Services	74,310
Department of the Interior	67,812
Department of Transportation	54,311
Department of Commerce	42,101
Department of Labor	15,379
Department of Energy	14,882
Department of State	11,142
Department of Housing and Urban Development	9,416
Department of Education	4,333
Subtotal: All cabinet departments	1,718,645
Independent Agencies	
Social Security Administration	60,465
Environmental Protection Agency	17,894
National Aeronautics and Space Administration	18,516
General Services Administration	11,826
All other independent agencies	58,144
Total	1,885,490

Source: OPM's FedScope database.

FEDERAL CIVILIAN EMPLOYMENT BY LOCATION

As of March 2008, about 97.5% of federal civilian employees worked in the United States. As shown in Table 5 below, more than 35% of federal civilian employees' duty stations (665,826 of 1,885,490) were in four states (California, Virginia, Texas, and Maryland) and the District of Columbia. DOD had the largest number of federal employees in 35 states, and the department had the second highest number of employees in eight other states and in the District of Columbia. DVA had the largest number of federal employees in 10 states, and was the second largest federal employer in 24 other states. Other federal departments or agencies with large numbers of employees in certain states included DHS (with more than 10,000 employees in five states, including more than 20,000 in both California and Texas); the Department of Justice (DOJ, with more than 21,000 employees in the District of Columbia); and the Department of Health and Human Services (HHS, with more than 32,000 employees in Maryland). Among independent agencies, the Social Security Administration was the largest and most ubiquitous, with more than 11,000 employees in Maryland, more than 1,000 employees in 15 other states, and an average of more than 350 employees in each of the remaining states.

As of March 2008, 34,578 federal civilian employees worked in foreign countries, 13,844 employees worked in U.S. territories, and 765 worked in "unspecified" locations.[12] As Table 6 below shows, more than 90% of federal civilian employees in foreign countries worked for DOD, with DHS and the Agency for International Development (AID) a distant second and third, respectively. DOD employees in foreign countries most commonly worked for the Army (11,653 employees) or in DOD "Education Activity" (10,615 employees).

More than 75% of federal employees in U.S. territories worked for DOD, DVA, or DHS. Within DOD, most employees worked for the Army (1,191 employees) or in DOD "Education Activity" (952 employees). Within DHS, most employees worked for either the Transportation Security Administration (TSA, 1,069 employees) or the Bureau of Customs and Border Protection (838 employees).

Table 5. States With Largest Number of Federal Civilian Employees (Duty Stations), March 2008

State	Federal Civilian Employees	Major Federal Employer(s)
California	152,554	DOD (55,238) DVA (21,886) DHS (20,119)
District of Columbia	149,034	DOJ (21,309)
Virginia	127,986	DOD (81,106)

State	Federal Civilian Employees	Major Federal Employer(s)
Texas	124,577	DOD (42,414) DHS (21,756)
Maryland	111,675	HHS (32,432) DOD (30,561)
Florida	78,436	DOD (25,409)
Georgia	72,621	DOD (33,626)
Pennsylvania	64,326	DOD (24,750)
New York	64,042	DVA (16,583)
Washington	50,052	DOD (24,547)
Illinois	46,177	DOD (14,110)
Ohio	45,685	DOD (21,852)
North Carolina	37,991	DOD (18,187)
Missouri	37,181	DOD (8,952)
Arizona	37,130	DOD (8,479)
Alabama	36,487	DOD (22,175)
Oklahoma	34,390	DOD (20,444)

Source: OPM's FedScope database.

Note: The table includes all states with at least 30,000 federal employees, and shows the largest federal employer in those states (including all departments with 20,000 or more employees in the state). For security purposes, FedScope does not provide detailed location information for certain agencies (e.g., the Federal Bureau of Investigation, the Drug Enforcement Agency, and the U.S. Secret Service). Employees of these agencies that work in the Washington, DC-MD-VA-WV Metropolitan Statistical Area are all reported as working in the District of Columbia. Other employees are reported as "Suppressed" (a total of 32,000 in the Department of Justice). As a result, FedScope somewhat overstates employment for the District of Columbia and understates employment for all states, territories, and foreign countries.

Table 6. Federal Civilian Employees in Foreign Countries and U.S. Territories by Major Department or Agency, March 2008

Department or Agency	Number of Federal Civilian Employees Working		
	Foreign Countries	U.S. Territories	Outside the United States
DOD	31,563	4,041	35,604
DVA	17	3,566	3,583
DHS	918	2,896	3,814
AID	909	0	909
USDA	186	723	909
Treasury	48	613	661
All other departments and agencies	937	2,035	2,972
Total	34,578	13,844	48,422

Source: OPM's FedScope database.
Note: FedScope does not include Foreign Service personnel in the Department of State.

Although there was at least one federal civilian employee in 162 foreign countries, Table 7 below shows that more than 75% of these employees worked in four countries — Germany, Japan, Korea, and Italy. In these countries, 99% of the employees worked for DOD. Federal employment in U.S. territories is even more stratified, with more than 75% of employees in those areas working in Puerto Rico and 93% working in either Puerto Rico or Guam. In Puerto Rico, the major agencies are DVA (3,566 employees), DHS (2,896 employees), and DOD (2,151 employees). In the other territories, DOD is the dominant agency (e.g., 697 of 720 employees in the Virgin Islands).

Table 7. Federal Civilian Employees in Foreign Countries and U.S. Territories by Major Countries and Territories, March 2008

Country/Territory	Federal Civilian Employees	
	Number	Percent of Total
Foreign Countries		
Germany	13,901	40.2%
Japan	7,013	20.3%
Korea	2,839	8.2%
Italy	2,368	6.8%
United Kingdom	1,748	5.1%
Iraq	777	2.2%
Belgium	632	1.8%
All other countries	5,300	15.3%
Total in foreign countries	34,578	100.0%
U.S. Territories		
Puerto Rico	10,605	76.6%
Guam	2,283	16.5%
Virgin Islands	720	5.2%
All other territories	236	1.7%
Total in U.S. territories	13,844	100.0%

Source: OPM's FedScope database.

CHANGES IN THE SIZE OF THE FEDERAL CIVILIAN WORKFORCE

As Figure 2 below indicates, the federal civilian workforce became somewhat smaller between 1998 and 2000, but has grown since 2000. As of March 2008, the workforce had about 75,000 more employees than it had in September 1998. As mentioned previously, though, the number of federal contractors is believed to have increased much more substantially during this period, growing by more than 3 million workers between 1999 and 2005 (from more than 4.4 million to more than 7.6 million).[13]

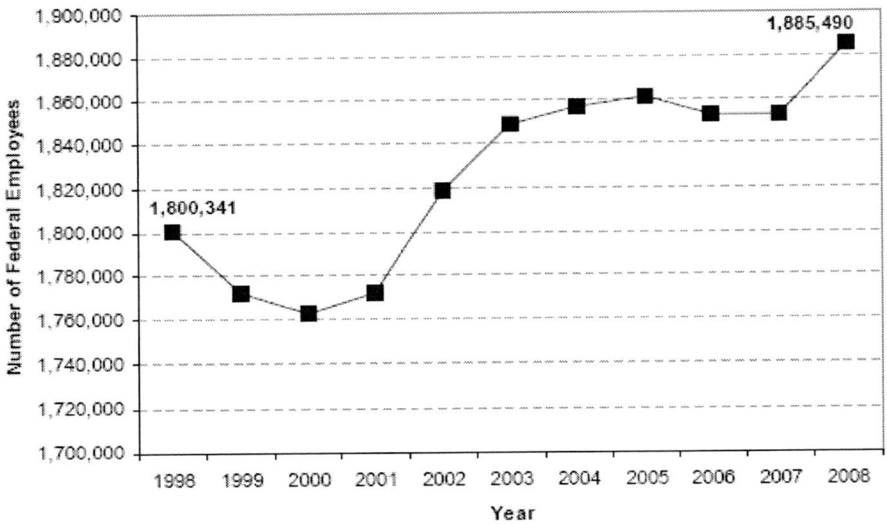

Source: OPM's FedScope database.

Figure 2. Size of the Federal Civilian Workforce, 1998 to 2008.

Several federal departments and agencies were created or substantially reorganized between 1998 and 2008, so tracking changes over time by department or agency must take those changes into account. For example, before DHS was created in 2003, several of its bureaus were parts of other cabinet departments (e.g., the U.S. Coast Guard was in the Department of Transportation, the U.S. Customs Service was in the Department of the Treasury, and the Immigration and Naturalization Service was in the Department of Justice).

With that caveat, Table 8 below shows the number of employees in the major departments and agencies in September 1998 and March 2008. As the table shows, some of the agencies that were unconnected to the creation of DHS grew larger during this period (e.g., HHS[14] and DVA), and some grew smaller (e.g., the Department of Agriculture and SSA).

Table 8. Federal Civilian Workforce: September 1998 and March 2008

Department/Agency	September 1998	March 2008	Change	
Department of Agriculture	107,709	95,513	(12,196)	(11.3%)
Department of Commerce	38,933	42,101	3,168	8.1%
Department of Defense	710,412	669,926	(40,486)	(5.7%)
Department of Justice	122,580	106,635	(15,945)	(13.0%)
Department of Labor	15,946	15,379		(3.6%)
Department of Energy	16,148	14,882	(1,266)	(7.8%)
Department of Education	4,833	4,333	(500)	(10.3%)
Department of Health and Human Services	58,261	74,310	16,049	27.5%
Department of Homeland Security	(Did not exist)	170,663	—	—
Department of Housing and Urban Development	9,984	9,416		(5.7%)
Department of the Interior	73,038	67,812	(5,226)	(7.2%)
Department of State	15,637	11,142	(4,495)	(28.7%)
Department of Transportation	64,858	54,311	(10,547)	(16.3%)
Department of the Treasury	141,966	118,555	(23,411)	(16.5%)
Department of Veterans Affairs	240,846	263,667	22,821	9.5%

Table 8. (Continued)

Department/Agency	September 1998	March 2008	Change	
EPA	19,242	17,894	(1,348)	(7.0%)
GSA	14,221	11,826	(2,395)	(16.8%)
NASA	19,207	18,516	(691)	(3.6%)
SSA	65,629	60,465	(5,164)	(7.9%)
All other independent agencies	70,891	58,144	(12,747)	(18.0%)
Total	1,810,341	1,885,490	75,149	4.2%

Source: OPM's FedScope database.
Note: Negative changes are in parentheses.

TYPES OF APPOINTMENTS AND WORK SCHEDULES

As Table 9 below indicates, almost 90% of federal employees in March 2008 were full-time, permanent employees (which was about the same percentage as in September 1998). About 5% of federal employees were full-time, nonpermanent; 3% were not full-time, permanent; and 3.5% were not full-time, nonpermanent.[15]

Table 9. Federal Employees' Type of Appointment and Work Schedule, March 2008

Work Schedule	Type of Appointment			
	Permanent	Non-permanent	Unspecified	Total
Full-time	1,664,642	96,089	117	1,760,848
Not Full-time	58,767	65,735	2	124,534

Work Schedule	Type of Appointment			
	Permanent	Non-permanent	Unspecified	Total
Unspecified	89	5	14	108
Total	1,723,528	161,829	133	1,885,490

Source: OPM's FedScope database.

The departments and agencies with the largest percentage of non-permanent employees were SSA (32.6%), HHS (28.6%), and the Department of State (24.3%). Those with the largest percentage of employees working less than a full-time schedule included OPM (22.6%), HHS (20.1%), and the Department of Commerce (18.0%). There were also substantial variations within these departments and agencies. For example, within the Department of Commerce, almost half (49.9%) of Census Bureau employees worked less than full-time; rates for the other parts of the department were less than 9%.

THE ARRIVAL AND DEPARTURE OF FEDERAL EMPLOYEES

In each of the last several years, about 250,000 employees joined federal agencies. These "accessions" may be divided into two main groups — employees who transferred into the agencies from other federal agencies (either through individual or mass actions) and new hires. Each year, transfers are typically less than 10% of all accessions.[16] In FedScope, "new hires" are divided into competitive selections, excepted service appointments,[17] and selections for the Senior Executive Service (SES). As Table 10 below indicates, in 2007 (the most recent year for which complete data are available), most new federal hires were into excepted service positions, not through the competitive selection process.

The table also shows, however, that most federal hiring in 2007 was for other than full-time and/or temporary employment. Of the 240,763 hires in 2007, less than half (107,113, or 44.5%) were full-time/permanent employees. Among these fulltime/permanent hires, 59,721 (55.8%) were hired through the competitive selection process and 47,061 (43.9%) were hired into excepted service positions. Some agencies were more prone to hire full-time, permanent employees without using the competitive selection process than others. For example, in 2007, 100%

of TSA hires and 90.5% of hires in the Bureau of Customs and Border Protection were into excepted service positions.[18]

In each of the last several years, about 250,000 employees separated from federal agencies in one of two ways — through transfers to other agencies (either through individual or mass actions) or via separations from federal service. As was the case with accessions, transfers typically account for about 10% of all separations each year.[19]

Table 10. Type of Federal Hiring by Type of Position, 2007

Type of Position	Type of Hiring			
	Competitive	Excepted Service	Senior Executive Service	Total
Full-time permanent	59,721	47,061	331	107,113
Not full-time permanent	36,622	96,998	30	133,650
Total	96,343	144,059	361	240,763

Source: OPM's FedScope database.

Table 11. Type of Separation From Federal Service by Type of Position, 2007

Type of Position	Type of Separation from the Federal Service					
	Quit	Retire	Removal	Death	RIF/ Other	Total
Full-time, permanent	42,120	60,515	8,649	2,788	746	114,818
Not full-time, permanent	46,553	1,729	57,453	254	380	135,961
Total	88,673	62,244	66,302	3,042	1,126	250,779

Source: OPM's FedScope database.

Separations from the federal service may be divided into employees who quit, retire, are separated through a reduction-in-force (RIF), are terminated, die, or have some other type of separation. As Table 11 above shows, the most common forms of separation from the federal service in 2007 were quits (40.0% of all separations from federal service), removals/terminations (29.9%), and retirements (20.1%). However, when considering only full-time, permanent employees, retirements were most common (52.7% of all separations from federal service) followed by quits (36.9%). Almost 87% of all removals/terminations involved employees who were not full-time, permanent employees.

CHANGES IN FEDERAL OCCUPATIONAL CATEGORIES

Federal occupations vary widely, from pipefitting to psychology.[20] At the broadest level, federal occupations are categorized as blue-collar and white-collar, and the white-collar occupations may be grouped into five general categories: professional, administrative, technical, clerical, and other.[21] Table 12 below shows the distribution of federal employees in these categories in 1998 and 2008. The table shows that the number of employees working in blue collar and clerical occupations declined substantially during this period (down 17.2% and 19.3%, respectively), while the number working in administrative occupations increased substantially (up 23.3%). The number of employees in professional occupations increased slightly (up 4.3%), and the number in technical occupations declined slightly (down 2.0%).

Table 12. Occupational Categories in the Federal Civilian Workforce, September 1998 and March 2008

Occupational Category	September 1998	March 2008	Change	
			Number	Percent
Blue-collar	242,977	201,272	(41,705)	(17.2)
White-collar	1,567,170	1,683,801	116,631	7.4
— Professional	439,704	458,475	18,771	4.3
— Administrative	531,395	655,175	123,780	23.3

Table 12. (Continued)

Occupational Category	September 1998	March 2008	Change	
— Technical	349,524	342,512	(7,012)	(2.0)
— Clerical	198,898	160,541	(38,357)	(27.6)
— Other	47,843	67,515	19,672	41.1
Total	1,810,341	1,885,490	75,149	4.2

Source: OPM's FedScope database.

Note: The "other" category includes a few hundred "unspecified" in each year. Negative changes are in parentheses.

CHANGES IN THE DEMOGRAPHIC CHARACTERISTICS OF THE FEDERAL CIVILIAN WORKFORCE

The federal civilian workforce has also changed during the last 10 years in terms of certain demographic characteristics (e.g., race/ethnicity, gender, age, and length of service). Some of those changes were more significant than others, and some appear to be continuations of longer-term trends.

Representation of Minorities and Women

Table 13 below provides data on the percentages of the federal civilian workforce in September 1998 and March 2008 that were minorities and women. The data indicate that the representation of minorities in the federal workforce rose somewhat during this period (from 29.6% to 33.1%), while the representation of women rose only slightly (from 44.4% to 44.7%). These data suggest a continuation of previous federal workforce trends. According to OPM, in September 1988, minorities composed 26.7% of the executive branch workforce, and women composed 42.2%.22

The relatively small change in the percentage of the federal workforce that was women between 1998 and 2008 may be partly a function of the decline in the number of federal clerical jobs during this period (down by more than 38,000, as shown in Table 13 above), and in their participation rate in those jobs. As Table

14 below shows, clerical jobs were 82% women in September 1998 but less than 70% women by March 2008. On the other hand, the representation of women in the professional and administrative categories (occupational categories that were growing during this period) increased somewhat during this period.

Table 13. Percentage of the Federal Civilian Workforce, Women and Minorities, 1998 and 2008

Women/Minorities	September 1998	March 2008
Women	44.4%	44.7%
Minorities	29.6%	33.1%
— African American	15.9%	17.6%
— Hispanic	6.4%	7.2%
— Asian/Pacific Islander	4.5%	5.4%
— Other minorities	2.1%	3.0%

Sources: The September 1998 data are from OPM's The Fact Book: 1999 Edition (OWI-99-2, September 1999), p. 56. The March 2008 data are from OPM's FedScope database.

Table 14. Percentage of Federal Civilian Workforce Categories That Were Women, 1998 and 2008

Occupational Category	Percentage of the Federal Workforce - Women	
	September 1998	March 2008
Blue-Collar	10.8%	11.0%
White-Collar	49.6%	48.7%
— Professional	39.0%	44.5%
— Administrative	42.6%	44.6%
— Technical	60.4%	59.4%

Table 14. (Continued)

Occupational Category	Percentage of the Federal Workforce - Women	
	September 1998	March 2008
— Clerical	82.1%	69.4%
— Other	12.2%	14.4%
Total	44.4%	44.7%

Source: OPM's FedScope database.

As Table 15 below shows, the percentage of the federal workforce that was minorities increased in all of the occupational groupings, but the increases were most notable in the professional, administrative, and "other" occupational categories.

Table 15. Percentage of Federal Civilian Workforce Categories That Were Minorities, 1998 and 2008

Occupational Category	Percentage of the Federal Workforce - Minorities	
	September 1998	March 2008
Blue-Collar	34.6%	34.8%
White-Collar	28.9%	32.9%
— Professional	21.3%	25.3%
— Administrative	24.5%	30.6%
— Technical	36.0%	39.7%
— Clerical	43.1%	46.4%
— Other	36.1%	41.0%
Total	29.6%	33.1%

Source: The September 1998 data are from OPM's The Fact Book: 1999 Edition (OWI-99-2, September 1999), p. 46 and p. 56. The March 2008 data are from OPM's FedScope database.

The Senior Executive Service represents the most experienced and senior element of the federal government's career workforce, and racial, ethnic, and gender diversity in the SES ranks can bring a variety of perspectives and approaches to policy development and implementation.[23] As Table 16 below shows, the percentage of the SES that was women in March 2008 was less than women's representation in the federal workforce as a whole (28.9% in the SES versus 44.7% in the workforce). Minorities were even less represented in the SES than in the federal workforce (15.3% of the SES were minorities versus 33.1% of the workforce as a whole).

Table 16. Percentage of the Federal Civilian Workforce and the Senior Executive Service That Were Women and Minorities, March 2008

Women/Minorities	Representation in the	
	Federal Workforce	SES
Women	44.7%	28.9%
Minorities	33.1%	15.3%
— African American	17.6%	7.9%
— Hispanic	7.2%	3.3%
— Asian/Pacific Islander	5.4%	2.4%
— Other minorities	3.0%	1.7%

Source: OPM's FedScope database.

Age and Length of Service

As Figure 3 below illustrates, the federal workforce was somewhat older in March 2008 than in September 1998. For example, the percentage of employees aged 55 and older increased from 15.1% in 1998 to 24.2% in 2008. On the other hand, the percentage of employees aged 30 to 49 declined from 59.5% in 1998 to 48.2% in 2008. These changes are evidence of a much-discussed aging of the federal workforce, with a larger percentage of federal employees potentially eligible to retire, or approaching retirement eligibility than in previous years.[24]

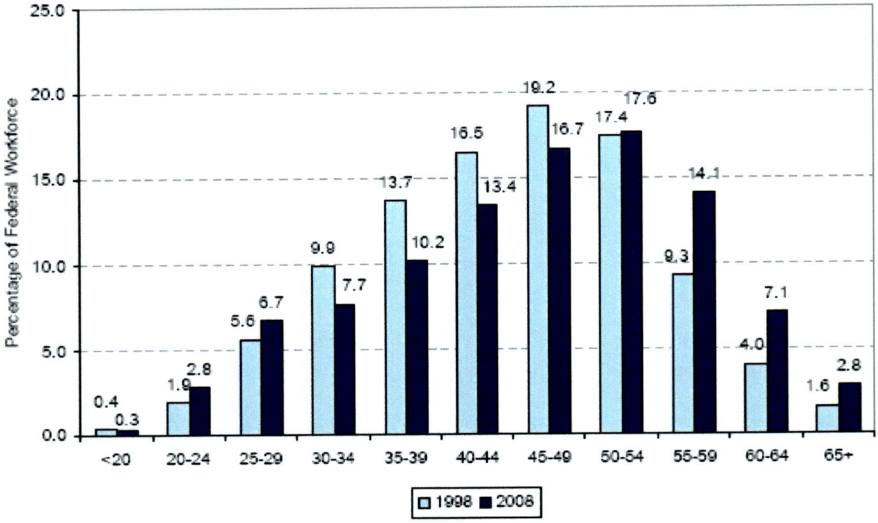

Source: OPM's FedScope database.

Figure 3. Age Distribution of the Federal Civilian Workforce, 1998 to 2008.

In contrast, the average length of service for the federal workforce declined between September 1998 and March 2008 — from 15.2 years to 14.7 years. As Figure 4 below shows, the changes between 1998 and 2008 were not uniform across the length-of-service categories. A larger percentage of the federal workforce had less than five years of federal service in 2008 than in 1998 (25.2% versus 15.8%, respectively), but a somewhat larger percentage of the workforce in 1998 also had more than 30 years of experience in 2008 (10.0% versus 6.8% in 1998). Differences between 1998 and 2008 are also apparent in the middle length-of-service categories (and particularly in the 10 to 14 year category). In 1998, 52.8% of the federal civilian workforce had between 5 and 19 years of service; by 2008, the percentage of the workforce with that category of service fell to 40.9%. The percentage of workers with between 10 and 14 years of service fell most sharply — from 19.6% in 1998 to 10.1% in 2008.

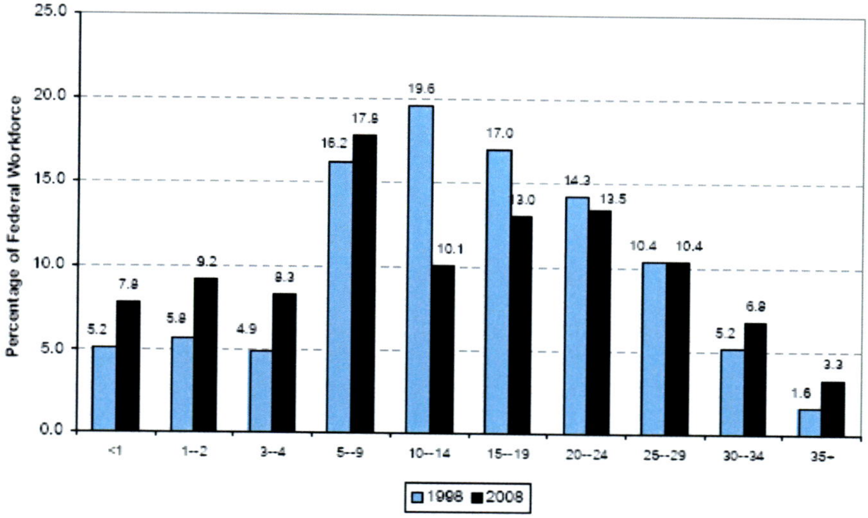

Source: OPM's FedScope database.

Figure 4. Years of Service Distribution of the Federal Civilian Workforce, 1998 to 2008.

Federal Civilian Workforce Pay Systems and Average Pay

The General Schedule (GS) was created by the Classification Act of 1949, and is by far the largest federal pay system. However, as Table 17 below shows, the percentage of federal civilian employees who were covered by the GS and related pay systems declined from nearly 80% in September 1998 to about 67% in March 2008, and the percentage in the "Prevailing Rate" (blue-collar) pay system declined from 13.4% to 10.6%. During the same period of time, the percentage of employees in single-agency pay systems increased substantially — particularly in pay systems not related to nursing or teaching. The number of employees covered by such systems increased from less than 16,000 in 1998 (0.8% of the federal civilian workforce) to more than 300,000 in 2008 (16.0% of the federal workforce). According to FedScope, within the "single agency" category, the largest pay plans (other than nursing) were

- the "Standard Career Group" pay schedules used by DOD for (1) professional and analytical employees (69,967 employees), (2)

supervisors and managers (35,355 employees), and (3) technical and support employees (20,873 employees);[25]

- the pay plan for TSA administrative employees within DHS, other than executives (59,918 employees);[26]
- the Federal Aviation Administration (FAA) "Core Compensation" plan (19,431 employees); and
- the FAA air traffic controller compensation plan (18,458 employees).

Table 17. Employees in Major Federal Civilian Pay Systems, 1998 and 2008

	September 1998		March 2008	
Federal Pay System	Number	Percent	Number	Percent
General Schedule or related	1,431,757	79.1%	1,264,913	67.1%
Prevailing Rate	241,837	13.4%	200,298	10.6%
Other	136,520	7.5%	420,217	22.3%
A. Government-wide	76,125	4.2%	69,830	3.7%
Admin Determined	58,652	3.2%	52,704	2.8%
Senior Executive Service	7,019	0.4%	7,550	0.4%
All other	10,454	0.6%	9,576	0.5%
B. Single Agency	60,395	3.3%	350,387	18.6%
Nursing	32,267	1.8%	40,024	2.1%
Teaching	12,242	0.6%	8,554	0.5%
All other	15,886	0.8%	301,809	16.0%
Total	1,810,341	100.0%	1,885,490	100.0%

Source: OPM's FedScope database.

As shown in Figure 5 below, if these rates of change continue into the future, by about the year 2020, GS and related pay systems could cover less than half of the federal workforce. By about the year 2026, the trend lines suggest that single agency pay systems may cover as many employees as the GS and related systems.

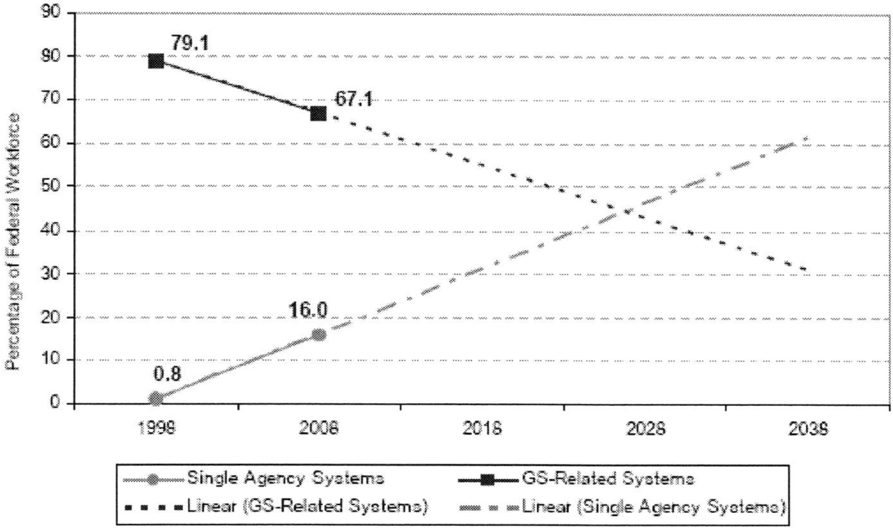

Source: OPM's FedScope database.

Figure 5. Percentage of Federal Civilian Employees in GS/Related and Single Agency Program Systems, 1998 to 2008 and Projections.

Average Salary Differences.

In March 2008, the average salary of the nearly 1.9 million federal employees covered by the CPDF was $69,061. However, this average varies substantially by agency and pay system, even among the major cabinet departments. For example, as Table 18 below shows, the average salary at DHS (which includes a large number of relatively lower-paid TSA employees) was $59,220, whereas the average salary at DOT (which includes a large number of relatively high-paid FAA employees) was $99,561.[27] The agency with the highest average salary in March 2008 was the Securities and Exchange Commission ($134,153), and the agency with one of the lowest average salary was the National Archives and Records Administration ($55,889).

Table 18. Average Salaries for Selected Federal Departments and Agencies, March 2008

Departments/Agencies	Average Salary (March 2008)
Departments/agencies with relatively high average salaries	
Securities and Exchange Commission	$134,153
Federal Housing Finance Board	$131,517
Commodities Futures Trading Corporation	$126,929
Merit Systems Protection Board	$111,750
Federal Labor Relations Authority	$110,139
Federal Communications Commission	$108,450
Nuclear Regulatory Commission	$108,085
Federal Deposit Insurance Commission	$105,457
Department of Transportation	$99,561
— Federal Aviation Administration	$101,368
Department of Energy	$97,243
Departments/agencies with relative low average salaries	
Department of the Interior	$62,736
— Indian Affairs	$49,623
Department of Agriculture	$60,968
— Agricultural Marketing Service	$44,777
Department of Defense	$64,735
— U.S. Army Installation Management	$53,599
Department of Homeland Security	$59,220
— Transportation Security Administration	$43,051
National Archives and Records Administration	$55,889

Source: OPM's FedScope database.

Average employee salaries also varied by major federal pay system, and sometimes within those pay systems. For example, as Table 19 below indicates, average salaries for employees in the blue-collar Prevailing Rate pay system were substantially lower than in the white-collar GS and related systems, and much lower than in the "other" systems (both government-wide and single-agency systems). However, the table also shows that there were substantial average salary differences by agency within the single agency systems (e.g., $43,576 for the pay systems within DHS versus $104,072 for the pay systems within DOT).

Table 19. Average Salaries Within Major Federal Pay Systems

Pay System/Department	Average Salary
General schedule/related pay systems	$68,674
Prevailing Rate pay system	$47,652
Other pay systems	$80,444
Government-wide pay systems	$104,856
Single agency pay systems	$75,628
Within DHS	$43,576
Within DOD	$77,012
Within DOT	$104,072

Source: OPM's FedScope database.

Another way to examine the salary differences by pay system is to look at the percentage of employees in each system above various pay points. As Table 20 below indicates, in the GS and related pay systems, less than 10% made more than $110,000 per year and less than 1% made more than $150,000 per year. On the other hand, more than 55% of employees in governmentwide pay systems (e.g., the Senior Executive Service and the physicians/dentist schedules) made more $110,000 per year, and more than one-third made more than $150,000 per year.

Table 20. Percentage of Federal Civilian Employees in Major Pay Systems at Various Pay Points, March 2008

Pay System	More than $110,000/year	More than $130,000/year	More than $150,000/year
General schedule/ related pay systems	9.7%	3.8%	0.8%
Other pay systems	20.8%	12.9%	6.6%
— Government-wide	55.2%	46.7%	34.1%
— Single agency	15.8%	8.1%	3.0%

Source: OPM's FedScope database.

SUMMARY OBSERVATIONS

The data provided in this report show that the size, shape, and character of the "federal workforce" varies substantially depending on how that workforce is conceived. Viewed broadly, the "federal government" includes civilian and military employees, all branches of government, and the U.S. Postal Service. However, most discussions of the federal workforce focus on civilian employees in the executive branch. Within that category, while OPM's FedS cope data indicates that nearly 90% of the workforce in March 2008 was composed of full-time, permanent employees, more than half of all accessions and separations each year involve temporary and/or other than full-time employees. Therefore, in discussions about "the federal workforce," or even more specific issues of federal recruitment and retention, it is important to be clear which agencies and what types of employees are included.

Some aspects of the federal civilian executive branch workforce are, however, relatively unambiguous. That workforce grew by more than 120,000 employees between 2000 (the low point during the last 10 years) and 2008, with the growth concentrated in homeland security-related agencies and DVA. The civilian workforce at DOD, on the other hand, declined between 1998 and 2008 by more than 40,000 employees (5.7%), and independent agencies like EPA and SSA also grew smaller. Although federal employees work in more than 100 agencies and organizations, the data indicate that nearly 60% of the federal civilian workforce was in three large cabinet departments in 2008 — DOD, DVA, and DHS. Even in its reduced size, DOD was by far the largest and most ubiquitous federal department or agency. In 35 states, DOD was the largest federal civilian employer (often by a wide margin), and DOD was the second largest employer in most of the other states. DOD also employed more than 90% of federal civilian employees in foreign countries (not including the foreign service).

It is also clear from the data that certain aspects of the federal workforce have changed in recent years. For example, between September 1998 and March 2008, the number of blue-collar jobs declined by more than 17%, and the number of clerical jobs declined by more than 27%. Meanwhile, the number of professional and administrative jobs increased by more than 4% and 23%, respectively. The percentage of the workforce that was minorities also increased during this period, but the percentage that was women remained almost constant. Also, although women as well as minorities represented an increasing proportion of the growing professional and administrative groups, their representation in the Senior Executive Service lagged behind their representation in the workforce as a whole.

The federal workforce is also noticeably older than it was 10 years ago. The percentage of the workforce that was age 55 or older rose by more than 60% between 1998 and 2008. In 1998, the age grouping with the largest percentage of federal workers was age 45-49; in 2008, the modal age grouping was age 50-54. With a larger percentage of federal workers either eligible or almost eligible to retire, OPM submitted a legislative proposal in March 2008 that would allow agencies in all three branches of government to more easily rehire annuitants without a salary offset. (Currently, unless agencies receive a waiver from OPM, federal retirees who are reemployed by the federal government must have their salaries reduced.) The proposal is similar to H.R. 3579, which would cover only executive branch employees. Other legislation has been introduced in the 1 10th Congress (e.g., H.R. 2780) that would allow certain employees to switch to a part-time schedule at the end of their career without affecting the calculation of their annuities.

The data also illustrate a decline in the dominance of the GS pay system during the last 10 years and a corresponding increase in the use of agency-specific pay systems. If recent trends continue into the future, the GS system will cover less than half of the federal workforce within the next 15 years, and the GS system will be surpassed by agency-specific pay systems shortly thereafter. Several of these single- agency pay systems are "pay for performance" systems, however, and those systems have been met with resistence from federal employees, unions, and some Members of Congress.[28] Therefore, to the extent that these single-agency systems are based on pay for performance, and to the extent that pay for performance is resisted by Congress and others, the growth in those agency-specific systems could slow in the future.

Perhaps the most surprising statistics, however, involve the "hidden" federal workforce of contractors and grantees. That workforce was estimated to include more than 10.5 million jobs in 2005 — more than more than twice as large as the combined total of all three branches of government, the U.S. Postal Service, the intelligence agencies, the armed forces, and the Ready Reserve. The number of contractor and grantee jobs was also estimated to have increased by more 50% between 1999 and 2005. If that rate of increase continued for the next six years, the number of federal contractors and grantees could reach nearly 16 million by the year 2011. However, the growth in contracting and grants could slow considerably if the next administration is not as committed to transferring certain federal functions to the private sector as the current Bush Administration.

REFERENCES

[1] U.S. Government Accountability Office, Human Capital: Transforming Federal Recruiting and Hiring Efforts, GAO-08-762T, May 8, 2008.

[2] U.S. General Accounting Office, High Risk Series: An Update, GAO-01-263, January 200 1.

[3] U.S. Office of Personnel Management, The Fact Book: 2005 Edition, p. 7, available at [https://www.opm.gov/feddata/factbook/2005/factbook2005.pdf]. OPM has not published The Fact Book since 2005, so 2004 data are the most recent available. Here and throughout this report, the number of employees reported is based on head counts of employees on board as of a particular date. Federal budget documents and other sources sometimes use "full-time equivalent" or "FTE" numbers, in which two employees working 20 hours per week are treated as one FTE.

[4] As the table shows, executive branch employment actually reached its lowest point during this period in 2000, and has risen somewhat since then.

[5] For more information on the Postal Service, see CRS Report RS22864, U.S. Postal Service Workforce Size and Employment Categories, 1987 - 2007, by Wendy Ginsberg.

[6] Pamela Hess, "Contractors Make Up One-Fourth of Intelligence Workforce," Government Executive.com, August 27, 2008. The "more than 100,000" estimate was verified by Ronald Sanders, chief human capital officer for the Office of the Director of National Intelligence.

[7] CRS Report RL34590, FY2009 National Defense Authorization Act: Selected Military Personnel Policy Issues, Lawrence Kapp, Coordinator.

[8] CRS Report RL3 0802, Reserve Component Personnel Issues: Questions and Answers, by Lawrence Kapp. In addition to the Ready Reserve, there were more than 21,000 members of the Standby Reserve and more than 650,000 members of the Retired Reserve.

[9] Paul C. Light, Robert F. Wagner Graduate School of Public Service, New York University, The New True Size of Government, August 2006. To view the study, see [http://wagner.nyu.edu/performance/files/True_Size.pdf].

[10] Ibid.

[11] Specifically, CPDF coverage of the executive branch currently includes all agencies except the Board of Governors of the Federal Reserve, the Central Intelligence Agency, the Defense Intelligence Agency, Foreign Service personnel at the State Department, the National Geospatial-Intelligence Agency, the National Security Agency, the Office of the Director of National Intelligence, the Office of the Vice President, the Postal Rate Commission, the Tennessee Valley Authority, the U.S. Postal Service, and the White House Office. Also excluded are the Public Health Service's Commissioned Officer Corps, non- appropriated fund employees, and foreign nationals overseas. The legislative branch is limited to the Government Printing Office, the U.S. Tax Court, and selected commissions.

[12] These data do not include certain agencies or employees in certain agencies (e.intelligence agencies and Foreign Service personnel in the Department of State).

[13] Paul C. Light, Robert F. Wagner Graduate School of Public Service, New York University, The New True Size of Government, August 2006.

[14] Most of the increase in HHS was in the Office of the Secretary, which grew from 2,896 in 1998 to 13,493 in 2008.The "non-permanent" category mainly consists of excepted service Schedule A and Schedule B employees. According to OPM, Schedule A appointing authorities "describe special jobs and situations for which it is impractical to use standard qualification requirements and to rate applicants using traditional competitive procedures." For example, agencies must use a Schedule A exception to hire attorneys because, by law, OPM cannot develop qualification standards or examinations for attorney jobs. OPM says Schedule B authorities "also apply to jobs and situations for which it is impractical to rate applicants using competitive procedures. However, under Schedule B authorities applicants must meet the qualification standards for the job. For example, Schedule B includes hiring authorities for the Student Temporary

Employment Program, the Student Career Experience Program, and the Federal Career Intern Program. Only students qualify for student programs; it is not practical to use competitive procedures for them." For more information, see[https://www.opm.gov/Strategic_ Management_of_ Human_Capital/fhfrc/FLX05020.asp# itemA1]. The "not full time" category mainly includes intermittent and part-time seasonal and nonseasonal employees.

[15] The "non-permanent" category mainly consists of excepted service Schedule A and Schedule B employees. According to OPM, Schedule A appointing authorities "describe special jobs and situations for which it is impractical to use standard qualification requirements and to rate applicants using traditional competitive procedures." For example, agencies must use a Schedule A exception to hire attorneys because, by law, OPM cannot develop qualification standards or examinations for attorney jobs. OPM says Schedule B authorities "also apply to jobs and situations for which it is impractical to rate applicants using competitive procedures. However, under Schedule B authorities applicants must meet the qualification standards for the job. For example, Schedule B includes hiring authorities for the Student Temporary Employment Program, the Student Career Experience Program, and the Federal Career Intern Program. Only students qualify for student programs; it is not practical to use competitive procedures for them." For more information, see [https://www.opm.gov/Strategic_ Management_ of_Human_Capital/fhfrc/FLX05020.asp# itemA1]. The "not full time" category mainly includes intermittent and part-time seasonal and nonseasonal employees.

[16] For example, in 2007, 22,781 (8.6%) of the 263,544 accessions were either individual or mass transfers. The exception to this trend in recent years was 2003, when more than 162,000 employees were mass transferred when DHS was created, including 67,958 at TSA, 37,416 at the Bureau of Immigration and Customs Enforcement, and 24,239 at the Bureau of Customs and Border Protection.

[17] Certain positions are excepted from competitive service by law, by executive order, or by OPM on the grounds that competitive examinations for such positions are not appropriate or impracticable (e.g., attorneys, medical doctors, and students under certain temporary employment programs).

[18] Several agencies have been granted broad excepted service hiring authority, including TSA, DHS, DVA, the Government Accountability Office, and the Federal Bureau of Investigation. See [ttp://www. makingthedifference.

org/federalj obs/exceptedservice.shtml] for a list of the major excepted service agencies.

[19] For example, in 2007, 29,392 (11.7%) of the 250,779 separations were either individual or mass transfers.

[20] As of March 2008, there were 2,645 federal employees in the "pipefitter" occupational series, and 5,125 employees in the "psychology" series.

[21] See [http://www.opm.gov/feddata/gp58.pdf] for the distinctions between these groups.

[22] U.S. Office of Personnel Management, The Fact Book, 1999 .Edition: Federal Civilian Workforce Statistics, OWI-99-2 (September 1999).

[23] See, for example, David W. Pitts, "Representative Bureaucracy, Ethnicity, and Public Schools: Examining the Link Between Representation and Performance," Administration and Society, vol. 39 (July 2007), pp. 497-527; and Morgen S. Johansen, "The Effect of Female Strategic Managers on Organizational Performance, Public Organization Review, vol. 7 (September 2007), pp. 269-280.

[24] See, for example, testimony of Nancy H. Kichak, Associate Director for Strategic Human Resources Policy, U.S. Office of Personnel Management, before the Subcommittee on the Federal Workforce, Postal Service, and the District of Columbia, Committee on Oversight and Government Reform, U.S. House of Representatives, May 20, 2008, available at [http://www.opm.gov/feddata/gp58.pdf].

[25] For more information on the DOD pay system, see CRS Report RL34673, Pay-forPerformance: The National Security Personnel System, by Wendy Ginsberg.

[26] For more information on the DHS pay system, see CRS Report RL3226 1, DHs 's Max-HR Personnel System: Regulations on Classification, Pay, and Performance Management Compared With Current Law, and Implementation Plans, by Barbara L. Schwemle.

[27] The average salary for TSA employees was $43,051, whereas the average salary for FAA employees was $101,368

[28] See, for example, Laura D. Francis, "Lawmakers Told of Inequities in Federal Pay But Urged to Reject Alternative Pay Systems," BNA Government Employee Relations Report, August 7, 2007, p. 910; and Brittany Ballenstedt, "Defense to Probe Fairness of Pay for Performance System," Government Executive, August 22, 2008.

In: Federal Workforce Trends
Editor: Claude R. Lewis
ISBN 978-1-60692-830-1

Chapter 2

OLDER WORKERS: FEDERAL AGENCIES FACE CHALLENGES, BUT HAVE OPPORTUNITIES TO HIRE AND RETAIN EXPERIENCED EMPLOYEES*

Barbara D. Bovbj and Robert N. Goldenkoff

WHY GAO DID THIS STUDY

The federal workforce, like the nation's workforce as a whole, is aging. As experienced employees retire, they leave behind critical gaps in leadership and institutional knowledge, increasing the challenges government agencies face in maintaining a skilled workforce. We and others have emphasized the need to hire and retain older workers as one part of a comprehensive strategy to address expected labor shortages. The Office of Personnel Management (OPM), as the government's central personnel management agency, is responsible for helping agencies manage their human capital.

The Chairman of the Senate Special Committee on Aging asked GAO to discuss (1) the age and retirement eligibility trends of the current federal workforce, (2) the strategies federal agencies are using to hire and retain older

* This is and edited, excerpted and augmented edition of an United States Government Accountability Office publication GAO-08-630T, dated April 30, 2008.

workers, and (3) our observations on how these strategies position federal agencies to engage and retain older workers.

To address these objectives, we analyzed demographic data from OPM's Central Personnel Data File, and interviewed officials at OPM and selected federal agencies.

OPM is taking action to address past recommendations related to better assisting agencies in using personnel flexibilities. GAO is making no new recommendations at this time.

WHAT GAO FOUND

Governmentwide, about one-third of federal career employees on board at the end of fiscal year 2007 are eligible to retire between now and 2012. Many of these workers are concentrated in certain agencies. For example, nearly half of employees on board at the end of fiscal year 2007 at the Departments of Housing and Urban Development and Transportation, and at the Agency for International Development and the Small Business Administration, will be eligible to retire by 2012. The proportion of workers eligible to retire is also expected to be high in certain occupations, including those considered mission critical, such as air traffic controllers and customs and border protection agents, where more than half of the employees will be eligible at that time. Retirement eligibility will be especially pronounced among the agencies' executives and supervisors—over 60 percent of career executives are projected to be eligible by 2012.

Federal agencies have a variety of flexibilities at their disposal to help them recruit and retain older workers, including using temporary hires to address short-term needs and rehiring retired federal workers. However, we found that agencies have not always been aware of the full range of available flexibilities. One agency we reviewed—the Social Security Administration—is particularly at risk of losing a substantial portion of its workforce to retirement and has used a variety of strategies to hire and retain older workers, including offering recruitment, retention, and relocation bonuses. Other agencies, such as the Environmental Protection Agency, have developed alternative approaches to attract experienced workers to meet their mission needs. Moreover, certain governmentwide flexibilities, such as flexible and part-time schedules, while not focused directly toward older workers, are particularly attractive to them.

Overall, the federal government already has a number of characteristics that appeal to all employees and is making progress toward becoming a model employer of older, experienced workers. For example, federal employees can telecommute, work flexible hours, and receive health and retirement benefits that older workers find especially attractive. OPM and Congress are taking steps to minimize some challenges that agencies face, but opportunities for improvement remain. For example, OPM has developed online decision support tools to provide agencies with guidance on how to use available hiring flexibilities and retention strategies. Congress has legislation pending that incorporates OPM's proposals to enhance agencies' ability to hire and retain older workers by giving agencies the authority, without OPM approval, to rehire retirees without penalty. Agencies have a shared responsibility to pursue the full range of flexibilities and authorities available and to communicate this information within their own agencies. Collectively, these measures will help make federal agencies more competitive in the labor market for all demographic groups.

Mr. Chairman, Ranking Member, and Members of the Committee:

Like the nation's workforce as a whole, the federal workforce is aging and ever larger proportions are nearing retirement eligibility. When they retire, these older, experienced workers may leave behind critical gaps in leadership, skills, and institutional knowledge. At the same time, the rate of growth for the pool of younger workers is declining, and by 2025 overall labor force growth is expected to be only one-fifth of what it is today and much less than the projected growth in the number of retirees. As a result, the federal government and other employers may face increased competition in hiring skilled workers, and unless they develop effective retention strategies, employers will need to look more aggressively for workers with the right skills to meet their needs.

Historically, the federal government has faced challenges hiring and retaining talented workers in key fields, and the looming retirement wave in federal agencies will only exacerbate these challenges. Older, experienced workers represent a large and underutilized national resource. Many experts maintain that older workers offer competitive advantages to employers because they often possess management and organizational skills that can be used in a variety of settings, and they bring to the job knowledge, experience, and productive work habits.[1] In addition, today's older workers are better educated and healthier, and are expected to live longer than previous generations. As the nation's largest employer, the federal government is well positioned to serve as a role model for other employers. As with private sector employers, efforts directed at recruiting, engaging, and retaining a diverse workforce, including older workers, may serve to make the federal government a more competitive and productive employer overall.

Because of this committee's continuing interest in older workers, we are especially pleased to be here today to discuss work that we have conducted at your request. In this work, we examined federal government efforts to tap the pool of older workers to meet its workforce needs. As requested, our testimony today, will discuss (1) the age and retirement eligibility trends of the current federal workforce; (2) the strategies federal agencies are using to recruit, hire, and retain older workers; and (3) our observations on how these strategies position federal agencies to engage and retain older workers.

To describe demographic trends relating to the retirement eligibility and aging of the federal workforce, we analyzed information on the 24 Chief Financial Officer Act (CFO) agencies from the Office of Personnel Management's (OPM) human resource reporting system, the Central Personnel Data File (CPDF).[2] Based on our previous work, we have determined that the CPDF is sufficiently reliable for the informational purpose of this testimony. In reviewing strategies federal agencies use to recruit, hire, and retain older workers, we interviewed officials in selected agencies, including the Departments of Agriculture, Housing and Urban Development (HUD), Labor, and State, as well as the Internal Revenue Service (IRS), Environmental Protection Agency (EPA), Nuclear Regulatory Commission (NRC), and the Social Security Administration (SSA). We chose these agencies because they had relatively large proportions of employees who were eligible to retire or because they were implementing different approaches to hiring and retaining older workers. In addition, we interviewed officials at OPM to obtain their perspective on government retirement trends, and how agencies can address them. For the purposes of this testimony, we define an older worker as an employee aged 55 or over. We conducted our work from November 2007 to April 2008 in accordance with generally accepted government auditing standards. Those standards require that we plan and perform the audit to obtain sufficient appropriate evidence to provide a reasonable basis for our findings and conclusions based on our audit objectives. We believe that the evidence we obtained provides a reasonable basis for our findings and conclusions. See appendix I for a detailed discussion of our scope and methodology.

In summary, the large proportion of federal workers who are eligible to retire now and will be in the near future presents challenges and opportunities for federal agencies. While the proportion of older workers eligible to retire varies across agencies, four agencies—Small Business Administration, the Agency for International Development, HUD, and the Department of Transportation—are well above the governmentwide average of 33 percent. Proportions of workers eligible to retire are projected to be especially high in certain occupations and in key leadership positions—64 percent of career executives are projected to be eligible by 2012. These trends underscore the importance of strategic workforce planning. As the government's human capital leader, OPM is responsible for helping agencies develop their human capital management strategies. Federal agencies have a range of flexibilities and authorities available that they may use to hire, engage, and retain workers. While only one of these flexibilities is largely focused on older workers—one that allows agencies to rehire retirees without offsetting the annuity—many, such as flexible and part time work schedules, are particularly appealing to older workers. One agency we reviewed—the Social Security Administration—is particularly at risk of losing a substantial portion of its workforce—at a time when it will experience unprecedented growth in demand for services. To deal with these losses, SSA has largely focused on using governmentwide authorities, including paying recruitment and retention bonuses for hard-to-fill positions and providing workplace flexibilities, such as flexible work schedules and alternative work sites. Other federal agencies are developing alternative approaches to hire and engage older workers. For example, the State Department maintains databases with information on retirees' skills and experience that it uses to identify individuals who may be able to assist when special needs arise, such as to provide tsunami relief for Indonesia. Overall, the federal government is making progress toward becoming a model employer of older, experienced workers. While there remain opportunities for improvement, OPM and the Congress are taking action to minimize the challenges agencies face in hiring and retaining older, experienced workers.

BACKGROUND

The percentage of older workers—those age 55 and older—is growing faster than that of any other age group, and they are expected to live and work longer than past generations. Labor force participation for this cohort has grown from about 31 percent in 1998 to 38 percent in 2007. In contrast, labor force participation of workers under age 55 has declined slightly. (See figure 1.)

Many factors influence workers' retirement and employment decisions, including retirement eligibility rules and benefits, an individual's health status and occupation, the availability of health insurance, personal preference, and the employment status of a spouse. The availability of suitable employment, including part-time work or flexible work arrangements, may also affect the retirement and employment choices of older workers.[3]

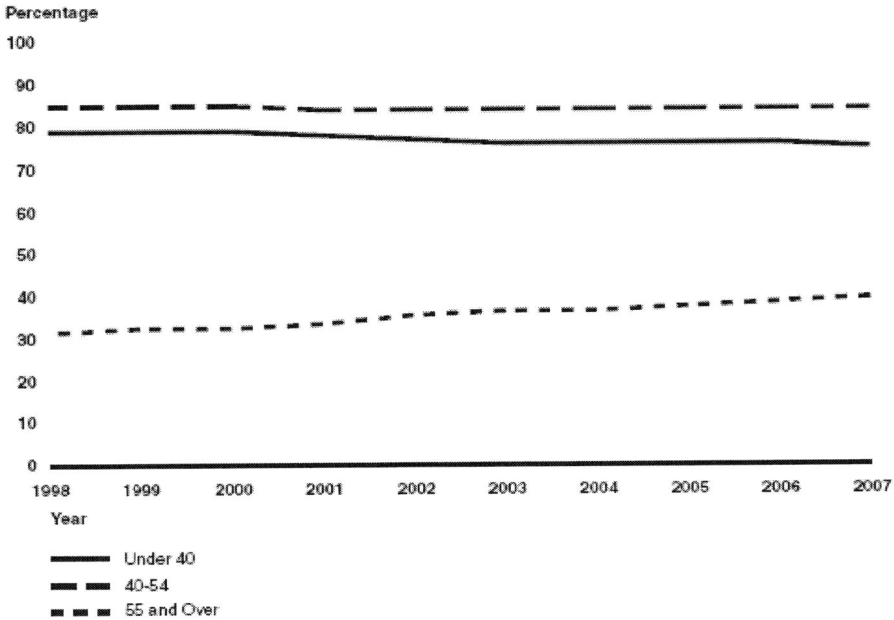

Source: GAO analysis of United States Bureau of Labor Statistics data.

Figure 1. Labor Force Participation of Workers under Age 40 to 55 and over.

As the government's human capital leader, OPM is responsible for helping agencies develop their human capital management systems and holding them accountable for effective human capital management practices. One such practice is strategic workforce planning, which addresses two critical needs: (1) aligning an organization's human capital program with its current and emerging mission and programmatic goals, and (2) developing long-term strategies for acquiring, developing, and retaining staff to achieve these goals. In developing these strategies, we have reported that leading organizations go beyond a succession-planning approach that focuses on simply replacing individuals. Rather they engage in broad, integrated succession planning and management efforts directed to strengthening both current and future organizational capacity.[4] In implementing its personnel policies, the federal government is required to uphold federal merit system principles in recruiting, engaging, and retaining employees. Among other provisions, the merit system principles require agencies to recruit and select candidates based on fair and open competition, as well as treat employees fairly and equitably. Federal agencies can recruit skilled or experienced workers, many of whom tend to be older, to fill positions requiring demonstrated expertise.

OPM is also responsible for administering retirement, health benefits, and other insurance services to government employees, annuitants, and beneficiaries. It develops implementing regulations when Congress makes new options available to federal employees and often takes the lead in advocating for new legislative options.

We and others have highlighted the need to hire and retain older workers to address the challenges associated with an aging workforce. In so doing, we have called upon the federal government to assume a leadership role in developing strategies to recruit and retain older workers. At our recommendation, Labor convened a task force composed of senior representatives from nine federal agencies[5] and issued its first report in February of this year.[6] The report provides information on strategies to support the employment of older workers, strategies for businesses to use that leverage the skills of an aging labor pool, individual opportunities for employment of older workers, and legal and regulatory issues associated with work and retirement. While the task force's focus was the private sector, some of the strategies it identified are relevant for federal agencies as well, for example, providing flexible work arrangements and customized employment options that include alternative work schedules and part time work.

The Growing Number of Retirement Eligible Employees in The Federal Workforce Highlight the Importance of Strategic Workforce Planning

As we and other organizations have previously reported, the federal workforce is aging, with an increasing number of employees eligible to retire.[7] Many of the workers who are eligible to retire in the 24 CFO agencies are in executive and supervisory positions, as well as in mission- critical occupations. These trends point to the importance of strategic workforce planning to help agencies forecast, with greater precision, who might retire, when they might retire, and the impact of their retirement on an agency's mission, and, using this information, develop appropriate strategies to address workforce gaps.

The percentage of older workers and workers nearing retirement eligibility varies across the federal government, with some agencies employing more such workers than others. For example, as shown in figure 2, the percentage of career federal employees in the 24 CFO agencies age 55 or older ranged from about 9 percent at the Department of Justice to about 38 percent at the Small Business Administration and Department of Housing and Urban Development in fiscal year 2007.

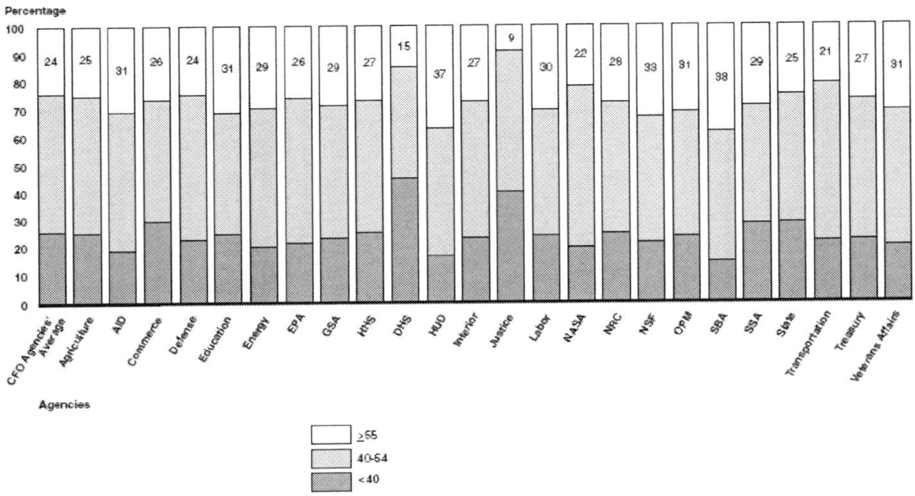

Source: GAO analysis of CPDF data.

Figure 2. Age Distribution of Career Federal Employees at CFO Agencies in Fiscal Year 2007

Importantly, about than one-third of federal workers will be eligible to retire over the next 5 years. Thirty-three percent of federal career employees on board as of the end of fiscal year 2007 will be eligible to retire during fiscal years 2008 through 2012. In comparison, about 20 percent of federal career employees on board as of the end of fiscal year 1997 were projected to be retirement-eligible during fiscal years 1998 through 2002.

Many workers projected to become retirement eligible by 2012 are concentrated in certain agencies. As figure 3 shows, the agency rates range from a low of 20 percent at the Department of Homeland Security (DHS) to a high of 46 percent at four agencies—the Agency for International Development (AID), the Department of Housing and Urban Development, the Small Business Administration (SBA), and the Department of Transportation (Transportation).

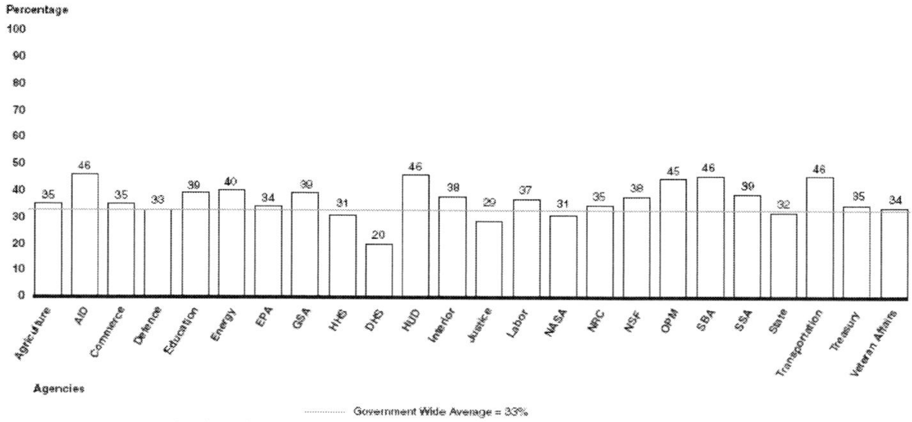

Source: GAO analysis of CPDF data.

Note: These data on retirement eligibility reflect the workforce as of the end of fiscal year 2007 and do not include actual or projected staff hiring or attrition at CFO agencies between 2007 and 2012. Some workforce turnover is common at federal agencies; however, in some cases more staff are leaving the agency than are being hired.

Figure 3. Percentage of Career Federal Employees Eligible to Retire by Fiscal Year 2012.

Estimated retirement eligibility rates will also likely vary at the component level—that is, by bureau or unit. Thus, even those agencies that have relatively low overall percentages of retirement eligible employees may have components that have higher percentages of retirement-eligible staff, which, in turn could affect the accomplishment of mission tasks and strategic goals for agency components and for the agency as a whole.

Certain occupations have particularly high rates of workers eligible to retire. As shown in figure 4, 50 percent or more of the workers in 24 of the 315 occupations with 500 or more staff we reviewed are eligible to retire by 2012. Several of these occupations, such as air traffic controllers, customs and border protection interdiction agents, and administrative law judges are considered mission critical. Federal law requires mandatory retirement at specified ages for some occupations, such as air traffic controllers who must retire at age 56.

Retirement eligibility will be especially pronounced among the agencies' executives and supervisors (see figure 5). Of the approximately 7,200 career executives as of the end of fiscal year 2007, 64 percent are projected to be retirement eligible by 2012, up from 41 percent in 2008. For supervisors who are not career executives, 45 percent will be eligible to retire by 2012.

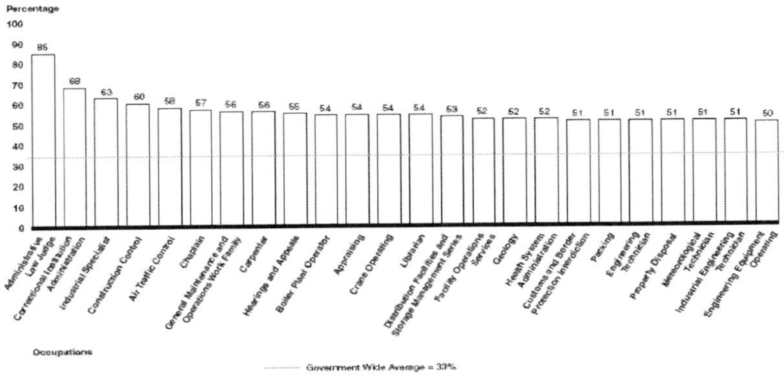

Source: GAO analysis of CPDF data.

Note: Retirement eligibility rates are for occupations with 500 or more employees as of the end of fiscal year 2007 that exceeded the governmentwide rate of 33 percent by 50 percent or more.

Figure 4. Certain Occupations with High Retirement Eligibility Rates by Fiscal Year 2012.

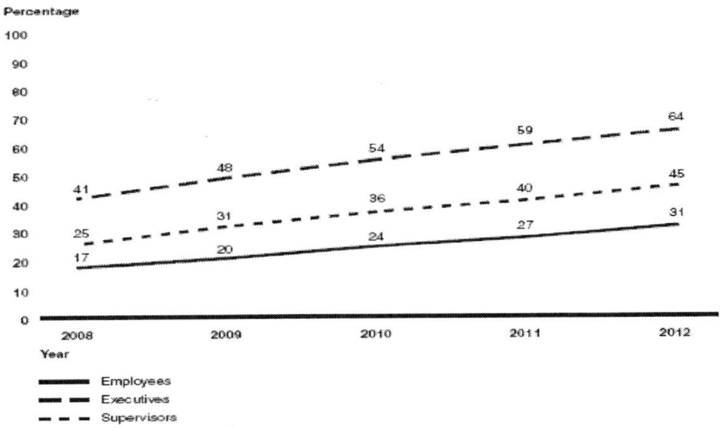

Source: GAO analysis of CPDF data.

Note: The term "executives" as used in this testimony includes political appointees above GS-15, those in the Senior Executive Service, those in the Senior Level and Senior Technical and Professional pay plans, and equivalent positions. The term "supervisor" as used in this testimony includes those whose duties involve assigning, directing, and supervising the work of others on a regular basis, as well as management officials who are not executives, but whose duties involve formulating agencies' policies.

Figure 5. Projected Retirement Eligibility Rates for Career Employees from Fiscal Years 2008 to 2012.

Although most federal employees do not retire immediately upon becoming eligible,[8] the increasing number of employees becoming retirement eligible in the near future points to the need for agencies to examine how these trends will affect them. In so doing, agencies should take into account location, occupation, and grade level of potential retirees, and develop appropriate succession planning strategies, which may include retaining older, experienced workers, to address the likely impact. At the same time, it will be important for agencies to consider their organization's strategic goals and the critical skills and competencies needed to meet future program outcomes, and to develop strategies to address any gaps in the number, skills, and competencies needed to achieve those outcomes.

Federal Agencies Have a Variety of Options Available to Hire and Retain Older Workers, but Some Federal Practices Make it Difficult to Use these Options

Federal agencies have a range of flexibilities at their disposal to help them engage and retain mission critical staff, including older, experienced workers. SSA, an agency that stands to lose a relatively large proportion of its experienced workforce in the upcoming retirement wave, is using many of the available governmentwide flexibilities to address workforce shortages. Some other federal agencies have developed alternative approaches that facilitate hiring and retaining older workers to meet their workforce needs. Despite the availability of recruitment, retention, and other flexibilities, agencies still face human capital challenges. In our past work, we found that agencies are not always able to make full use of available flexibilities, in part because they did not fully understand them.

OPM's Human Capital Policies and Guidance are Aimed at Attracting and Retaining a Diverse Workforce

As the government's human capital leader, OPM sets human capital policies for federal agencies. In many cases, OPM serves as the gatekeeper by approving or disapproving an agency's request to use some hiring authorities or other flexibilities. Other authorities do not require OPM's approval. [9] While only one of the available flexibilities is largely focused on older workers—dual compensation waivers—many, such as flexible and part time work, are particularly appealing to older workers. OPM does not specifically target older workers in its policies. Instead, efforts are focused on workers who possess the right skills and experience to meet agencies' workforce needs, without regard to age.

Governmentwide Hiring Authorities. Under existing rules and regulations, agencies have the authority to use a number of different approaches to hire workers, including older workers, without obtaining OPM approval. Among other approaches, they include using

- temporary appointments for short-term needs;[10]
- temporary assignees from state and local governments, colleges and universities, Indian tribal governments, and qualified not-for-profit agencies under the Intergovernmental Personnel Act (IPA);[11]
- commercial recruiting firms and nonprofit employment firms;[12]
- consultants for temporary or intermittent employment;[13]
- contractual arrangements: commercial temporary help for brief periods of time, and contracts for services, as long as the contracts follow federal procurement regulations.[14]

Agencies can also use additional hiring authorities by obtaining OPM's approval or by notifying OPM on a case-by-case basis of their intent. These include the following:

- Dual compensation waivers[15] to rehire federal retirees—OPM may grant waivers allowing agencies to fill positions with rehired federal annuitants without offsetting the salaries by the amount of the annuities. Agencies can request waivers on a case-by-case basis for positions that are extremely difficult to fill or for emergencies or other unusual circumstances. Agencies can also request from OPM a delegation of authority to grant waivers for emergencies or other unusual circumstances. These waivers by their nature are largely for older workers;[16]
- Special authority to hire for positions in contracting— agencies can rehire federal annuitants to fill positions in contracting without being required to offset the salaries. Agencies are required only to notify and submit their hiring plans to OPM;[17]

> The Internal Revenue Service (IRS) uses its dual compensation waiver to bring back retired Revenue Agents to train less experienced agents— an effective way, officials say, to pass down critical knowledge without pulling experienced employees away from their primary focus—auditing tax returns

- On-the-spot hiring without competition—this may be used in circumstances where (1) public notice has been given and (2) OPM has determined there is a severe shortage of candidates or a critical hiring need, such as in certain medical or information security occupations, or occupations requiring fluency in Middle Eastern languages;[18]
- Veterans' recruitment appointment—agencies may hire certain veterans without competition to fill positions up to the GS-11 level or for disabled veterans at any level;[19]
- Enhanced annual leave computation—agencies may credit relevant private sector experience when computing annual leave amounts.[20]

Flexible Schedules and Workplaces. Flexible schedules and workplaces are often extremely important to older workers. For example, some research indicates older workers want to set their own hours and to be able to take time off to care for relatives when needed.[21] In addition, older workers nearing retirement may prefer a part-time schedule, for example, as a means to retire gradually. Federal agencies have work schedule flexibilities that they can provide to their workers without prior approval from OPM. These include

- Part-time schedules—allow employees to work on a part-time basis; however, part-time work late in a career may result in a lower retirement annuity and may affect other benefits.[22]
- Flexible work schedules—allow full-time or part-time employees to determine their hours of work within established parameters or modify the typical work schedule of 8 hours a day, 5 days per week by, for example, permitting schedules of 10 hours per day, 4 days per week.[23]
- Alternative work sites—allow employees to work from home or outside the traditional office.[24]

> As part of a strategy to attract experienced workers away from highly paid private sector jobs, the Nuclear Regulatory Commission (NRC) offers its employees enhanced workplace flexibility, including the options of working from home and of setting alternative work schedules. Officials report that these options have sometimes been pivotal in convincing older workers to come to work for NRC.

Compensation Flexibilities. Agencies also have authority to provide additional compensation to employees. These include

- giving recruitment, relocation, and retention incentives to employees;[25]
- raising the pay rate of critical positions in an agency (requires OPM approval after consultation with OMB);[26]
- providing certain eligible physicians allowances of up to $30,000 per year. This flexibility requires OMB approval;[27] and
- using special rates, premium pay, and other compensation flexibilities to recruit and retain specified health care employees, under a delegation agreement with OPM.[28]

A Case Study: How One Agency Uses Available Flexibilities to Address a Looming Retirement Wave

One of the agencies we reviewed—the Social Security Administration (SSA)—is particularly at risk of losing a substantial portion of its workforce at a time when it will experience unprecedented growth in demand for its services. SSA faces looming shortages particularly in some mission critical positions, despite enhancing its human capital planning efforts. The agency is experiencing service delays, even at current staffing levels. For example, SSA had over 750,000 disability claims awaiting a decision at the hearing level at the end of January 2008, leading to an average waiting time in fiscal year 2008 of almost 500 days. These backlogs could increase in the future, given SSA's demographic profile. Indeed, according to SSA's data,[29] about 40 percent of its current workforce will be eligible to retire by 2012, and by 2017 that proportion will grow to more than half. The prospects for hiring new employees to replace retirees over this timeframe remains unclear. According to SSA officials, while the fiscal year 2008 budget provided sufficient funding to allow SSA to replace all of the employees that leave—and to add additional employees in some areas—budgetary constraints have prevented the agency from hiring enough new workers in the past and future hiring will depend upon the resources available. Even when SSA can hire, the agency faces stiff competition from the private sector, especially for jobs in the accounting, legal, and information technology fields.

The potential impact of retirements varies across the agency and will affect occupations SSA deems critical. By 2012, the proportion of those eligible to retire will generally range from 25 percent to 59 percent across such occupations. However, the proportion of administrative law judges eligible to retire is far higher—about 86 percent will be eligible by 2012 and nearly all by 2017. Moreover, SSA stands to lose a substantial portion of its leadership staff. Of its 138 Senior Executive Service (SE S) members, 62 percent are now eligible to retire and nearly 80 percent will be eligible by 2012. Of the over 6,000 supervisors, nearly 39 percent are currently eligible to retire and 57 percent could retire by 2012.

SSA has increasingly used information technology solutions in an effort to improve its human capital management. For example, to better understand where to place its human capital emphasis, SSA has developed an approach that uses historical data to project future retirements. The model projects who is likely to retire, and SSA uses these projections to estimate gaps in mission-critical positions and to identify regional and headquarters components most affected. With these estimates the agency develops action plans focused on recruiting and hiring, retention, and staff development. SSA has also developed user-friendly automated tools to help job applicants complete the applications process. This system keeps both applicants and managers advised of where the application is in the process.

SSA has used a variety of strategies to hire and retain older workers, some of which include the human capital flexibilities available to all federal agencies. For example, SSA offers recruitment, relocation, and retention bonuses to individuals with needed skills and considers an employee's private sector experience when computing annual leave status. The agency also offers workplace flexibilities, such as alternative work sites and flexible work schedules, seminars on dependent care for elderly family members and children, and learning opportunities such as midcareer and pre-retirement seminars. In addition, SSA provides the options of a phased retirement program—allowing employees to work on a part time basis during the years immediately prior to retirement—and a trial retirement program—allowing workers to return to work within a year of retiring if they repay the annuity they've received. However, SSA officials told us that the programs have been rarely used because of the financial penalty workers would face.

Under a delegation of authority from OPM, SSA has used dual compensation waivers to hire experienced retirees to fill staffing shortages in critical areas when these shortages constituted an emergency. From November 2000 through December 2006, SSA used this authority to rehire nearly 1,300 federal annuitants who were knowledgeable and proficient at processing complex, difficult workloads and who needed little or no training to fill mission critical workforce gaps.[30] This waiver authority expired in 2006 and was not renewed. However, SSA has been granted a waiver to reemploy administrative law judges to help reduce the disability hearings backlog. In addition, SSA was granted a waiver to rehire federal annuitants to provide relief in areas affected by hurricanes Katrina and Rita. SSA officials reported that when they have been allowed to use dual compensation waivers, their experiences were extremely positive.

Beyond using existing flexibilities, SSA has developed recruitment efforts that reach out to a broader pool of candidates, some of whom are older workers. For example, SSA began recruiting retired military and disabled veterans in 2002 because of its commitment to helping veterans. SSA is also beginning to reach out to older workers in order to achieve its diversity goal of attracting a multigenerational workforce. These steps have included developing recruiting material featuring images of older and younger workers.

Other Federal Agencies Have Developed Alternative Approaches to Hire and Engage Older Workers to Meet their Workforce Needs

In addition to SSA, we interviewed officials in several other agencies and learned that some have developed their own approaches to hiring and engaging older workers.

Identifying and recruiting retirees with critical skills by using technology. The Department of State has developed two databases to match interested Foreign Service and Civil Service retirees with short- term or intermittent job assignments that require their skill sets or experiences. One database—the Retirement Network, or RNet— contains a variety of information, including individuals' job experiences, foreign language abilities, special skills, preferred work schedule, and favored job locations. To identify individuals with specific skill sets, officials match information from RNet with another database that organizes and reports all available and upcoming short- term job assignments. For instance, in 2004, the agency identified current and retired employees familiar with Sumatra's culture and language and sent many of them to Indonesia to help with the tsunami relief efforts. According to officials, this technology has allowed them to identify individuals with specialized skills and specific job experience within hours. Before these systems were in place, the search for specific individuals would have taken days or weeks, and even then, the list of individuals would have been incomplete. Because different personnel rules apply to Foreign Service and Civil Service positions, the agency typically brings Civil Service retirees on as contractors—nonfederal employees without any reduction to earnings or annuities—and may hire Foreign Service retirees as federal employees who may earn their full salaries and annuities.[31]

Hiring older workers through nonfederal approaches. The Environmental Protection Agency (EPA) has designed a program that places older workers (55 years and over) in administrative and technical support positions within EPA and other federal and state environmental agencies nationwide. Instead of hiring older workers directly into the government as federal employees, EPA has cooperative agreements with nonprofit organizations to recruit, hire, and pay older workers. Under these agreements, workers are considered program enrollees, not federal employees. EPA's Senior Environmental Employment (SEE) program started as a pilot project in the late 1970s, and was authorized by the Environmental Programs Assistance Act in 1984.[32] According to EPA, many SEE enrollees come from long careers in business and government service, offer valuable knowledge, and often serve as mentors to younger coworkers. Depending on their skills and experience, program enrollees' wages vary, starting at $6.92 per hour and peaking at $17.29 per hour. Using the SEE program as a model, the Department of Agriculture's Natural Resources Conservation Service (NRCS) recently developed a pilot project called the Agriculture Conservation Enrollees/Seniors (ACES) program.[33] Officials from both EPA and NRCS told us that their programs are crucial in helping agencies meet workload demands and providing older workers with valuable job opportunities.

- Partnering with private firms to hire retired workers. In partnership with IBM and the Partnership for Public Service, the Department of the Treasury is participating in a pilot project that aims to match the talent and interest of IBM retirees and employees nearing retirement with Treasury's mission-critical staffing needs. Working together, the three organizations are designing a program that intends to send specific Treasury job opportunities to IBM employees with matching skill sets and experience; help create streamlined hiring processes; provide career transition support, such as employee benefits counseling and networking events; and encourage flexible work arrangements. Officials are developing the pilot project within existing governmentwide flexibilities that do not require special authority from OPM. As one official suggested, designing such a project may reveal the extent to which existing federal flexibilities allow new ways of hiring older workers.

- Engaging older workers through mentoring. Three of the agencies we spoke with are in the beginning stages of formalizing mentoring programs, recognizing that mentoring relationships help pass down knowledge to less experienced workers as well as engage older workers. According to one official at NRC, fostering mentoring relationships is essential for his agency. Not only do these relationships help to transfer knowledge to less experienced workers, they also help senior-level staff build strong professional relationships with junior employees.

Several Challenges Exist to Hiring and Retaining Older Workers in the Federal Government

Despite the availability of recruitment, retention, and other flexibilities, agencies still face human capital challenges. In our past work, we found that agencies were not always able to make full use of available flexibilities, in part because they did not fully understand the range of flexibilities at their disposal and did not always educate managers and employees on the availability and use of them. In addition, we found that inadequate funding and weak strategic human capital planning contributed to the limited use of these flexibilities. Moreover, OPM did not take full advantage of its ability to share information about when, where, and how the broad range of flexibilities are being used and should be used to help agencies meet their human capital management needs.

Several federal hiring procedures can also pose challenges and make it difficult for the federal government to compete with private sector employers. Cumbersome federal hiring procedures can make it difficult for older workers, as well as all other applicants, to get a federal job. Recently, the Partnership for Public Service reported that older workers face a number of challenges to getting a federal job. Many of the issues they raise affect applicants of all age groups. For example, for many of the jobs open to the public, too little time was allowed between the time the job was announced and the deadline for submitting a complete application. For this and other reasons, a majority of older workers they surveyed thought that applying for a federal job is difficult. To address the cumbersome and complicated federal hiring process, the report recommended that federal agencies publicize federal jobs beyond the internet, make federal job announcements and the application process more user-friendly, and keep applicants informed of their application status.[34]

Furthermore, the dual compensation rule, which requires annuitants' salaries to be offset by the amount of the annuities they receive, can create a financial disincentive for retirees wishing to return to federal service. Unless federal agencies receive authority to grant waivers of this rule, retired federal workers—unlike private sector or military retirees—would be working for reduced rates of pay. Other rules make it difficult to use flexibilities. For example, federal employees close to retirement may face reductions in the monthly retirement benefit if they choose to work parttime—or use a phased retirement approach—near the end of their careers.

FEDERAL EMPLOYMENT HAS A NUMBER OF ATTRIBUTES ATTRACTIVE TO OLDER WORKERS

Overall, the federal government is making progress toward becoming a model employer of older, experienced workers. Research has identified characteristics of work environments that older workers value that can serve as a model for federal agencies as they seek to hire and retain older workers. While there remain opportunities for improvement, OPM and Congress are taking action to minimize the challenges faced in hiring and retaining older, experienced workers.

OPM and Congress are Taking Steps to Minimize Challenges

As we discussed earlier, individual agencies have strategies that they can use to address some challenges to employing older workers, but actions from OPM, as the government's human capital leader, and Congress play pivotal roles in changing the landscape of rules regarding federal employment.

OPM has taken steps to provide agencies with guidance on how to use available flexibilities and authorities. For example, in the fall of 2005, OPM put a hiring flexibilities decision support tool online to assist agencies in assessing which flexibilities would best meet their needs. This Hiring Flexibilities Resource

Center provides in-depth information on a variety of flexibilities, including Direct Hire and Excepted Service. In January 2008, OPM updated its handbook on federal flexibilities and authorities, also online, which provides more information on both recruiting and retention strategies agencies can use to promote the positive aspects of the federal government. Responding to past findings about the length of time it takes to hire new employees, OPM has established a strategic goal to improve recruitment and retention, including faster hiring, hiring more veterans, rehiring annuitants, and faster application processing.

OPM has also encouraged federal agencies to consider a broad spectrum of employees as they seek to meet workforce needs. According to OPM, federal human capital managers are facing increasing competition in attracting and retaining talent. To meet this challenge, OPM has developed a new approach, called the Career Patterns initiative, for bringing the next generation of employees into federal positions. In its Career Patterns guidance to agencies, OPM identifies, among other things, scenarios that describe the particular characteristics of 10 types of individuals, including students, new professionals, experienced professionals, and retirees who could help broaden the pool of potential employees for federal jobs.

OPM has also recently proposed legislation to Congress that would enhance agencies' ability to hire and retain older workers. One proposal would give agencies the authority to grant dual compensation waivers without having to obtain OPM approval. The proposal calls for a yearly and lifetime limitation on how many hours an individual can be reemployed. A second proposal would increase the ability of employees to work on a part time basis during their pre-retirement years by changing the way the CSRS annuities based on part time services are computed.

Congress has taken action to address the retirement risks in selected occupations. For example, in 2006, Congress enacted legislation allowing federal agencies to hire federal retirees to fill acquisition-related positions without requiring annuity offset.35 The authority to use this provision expires on December 31, 2011. Agencies are required to consult with OPM and OMB in developing their plans for reemploying annuitants in acquisition-related positions and to submit their plans to OPM. OPM officials indicated that they have reviewed and approved 9 agencies' plans for consistency with the statutory criteria for reemploying annuitants in those positions. In addition, bills incorporating OPM's proposals related to dual compensation waivers and part time employment are currently pending in Congress.[36]

FEDERAL EMPLOYMENT ALREADY HAS A NUMBER OF CHARACTERISTICS APPEALING TO OLDER WORKERS AND OTHER EMPLOYEES

Although the availability of flexibilities generally varies by agency, agencies already have the authority to offer a number of the flexibilities and practices older workers find appealing in an employer. For example, AARP—one of the largest interest groups for individuals age 50 and older—developed criteria to evaluate an organization's performance in recruiting, engaging, and retaining this cohort and has, since 2001, used these criteria to identify the best employers for workers over 50.[37] Features of these criteria, as described by AARP, overlap with many of the flexibilities that federal employment offers. Their availability and usage in the federal government are shown in table 1.

Table 1. AARP's Criteria for Selecting the Best Employers for Older Workers and Their Usage in Government

AARP Criteria for selecting the best employers for older workers	Availability and usage by federalagencies
Recruiting Advertise in publicationsthat target diverse age groups; Develop recruiting material that appealsto workersof all ages	Available; usage variesby agency
Training opportunities Provide opportunitiesfor training, continuouseducation/learning, and career development	Available; usage variesby agency
Alternative work arrangements Provide for flexible hours, telecommuting, and phased retirement	Available; usage variesby agency
Benefits, including health and retirement Provide for health benefits, including the percentage of the premium that workersare required to pay and whether they are offered to part-time employees; long-term care insurance; defined benefit or defined contribution retirement plans	Available governmentwide

Source: AARP and GAO analysis.

One area where the government is particularly strong is the availability of health benefits. Federal agencies offer health benefits and pay a sizable portion of the cost. Health insurance may be an especially attractive recruitment and retention tool to older workers since employees generally need only 5 years of federal service with health insurance while employed to carry that benefit into retirement. The federal government also offers retirement benefits and life insurance, and provides the opportunity for employees to purchase long-term care insurance.

In other areas, agencies generally have the authority to offer a particular practice, but their actual usage varies by agency depending on the agency's needs, the nature of the work and other factors. For example, with respect to alternative work arrangements, the federal government offers a number of programs that help employees balance their personal and professional responsibilities, including telecommuting, part time employment, and flexible schedules.

Concluding Observations

A looming retirement wave could result in a possible "brain drain" for federal agencies unless they employ effective succession planning strategies—strategies that include hiring younger workers as well as retaining older workers who possess needed talents and skills and who can share these talents and skills with the next generation. Importantly, the government already has a number of tools in its human capital tool kit that provide agencies with flexibility they need to recruit and retain older workers. Moreover, federal employment offers a range of benefits and employment flexibilities, such as the availability of part-time employment that can make these jobs particularly attractive to older workers, as well as all demographic groups.

Still, while the federal government is making progress toward becoming a model employer of older workers, opportunities for improvement remain. First, our demographic analysis shows that while the federal workforce is aging, and an increasing number of employees will become eligible for

retirement in the coming years, these trends will have varying degrees of impact within particular agencies. As a result, it will be important for agencies to fully understand and forecast the implications of these trends so they can implement timely and appropriate succession strategies. Second, as certain federal agencies have developed alternative approaches to hire and engage older workers, it will be important for agencies to share lessons learned from these practices governmentwide. And third, despite the availability of employment flexibilities and practices that allow employees to balance their professional and personal responsibilities, individual agencies do not always take advantage of them.

Consequently, it is incumbent upon OPM to continue to work with federal agencies to help ensure they have (1) the flexibilities they need to attract and retain a diverse workforce that includes older workers; (2) the awareness of these flexibilities, as well as guidance and technical assistance needed to implement them; and (3) mechanisms to share best practices and lessons learned in attracting and retaining older workers. Becoming a model employer is a shared responsibility and it will be important for agencies to, among other actions, take advantage of available flexibilities and guidance on their use and communicate this information throughout the agency. Collectively, these measures will help make federal agencies more competitive in the labor market for all demographic groups.

Mr. Chairman, Ranking Member, and Members of the Committee, this concludes our prepared statement. We would be pleased to respond to any questions that you may have.

Appendix I. Scope and Methodology

Our objectives were to describe (1) the age and retirement eligibility trends of the current federal workforce; (2) the strategies federal agencies are using to recruit, hire, and retain older workers; and (3) our observations on how these strategies position federal agencies to engage and retain older workers.

Demographic Trends

To describe demographic trends relating to the retirement eligibility and aging of the federal workforce, we analyzed information on the 24 CFO agencies from OPM's human resource reporting system, the Central Personnel Data File (CPDF). We analyzed data on the age, retirement eligibility, occupations, projected retirement rates, and other characteristics of the career federal workforce. We used the following variables: agency, occupation, date of birth, service computation date, pay plan/grade, and supervisory status. All these variables were 97 percent or more reliable. Using the CPDF information, we analyzed the age distribution of career federal employees at CFO agencies by age groupings (under 40, 40-54, and 55 and over). We also analyzed the percentage of career federal employees on board at the end of fiscal year 2007, who would be eligible to retire from fiscal years 2008 to 2012, and the percentage of workers eligible to retire in occupations where the retirement rates exceeded the governmentwide average. As a proxy for those occupations that may be at risk due to high retirement eligibility rates, we selected occupations with 500 or more employees as of the end of fiscal year 2007 that exceeded the governmentwide rate of 33 percent by 50 percent or more. For this report, we defined older workers as those 55 and older.

Strategies Available to Federal Agencies to Hire and Retain Older Workers

To address this objective, we reviewed strategies available to federal agencies to hire and retain older workers through governmentwide hiring authorities and other flexible arrangements, we interviewed officials at OPM and other selected federal agencies, including Labor, and we reviewed previous GAO work relating to older workers and federal human capital strategies. We also reviewed relevant laws, literature on hiring and retaining older workers, and documents on federal human capital flexibilities. As a case study, we selected the Social Security Administration (SSA), to describe the strategies that one federal agency has taken to hire and retain older workers. We selected SSA because it is at high risk of losing a large proportion of mission-critical employees and because it risks losing these employees at the same time the need for its services will peak.

We interviewed human capital officers at selected agencies to collect such information as:

- the extent to which agency officials think they will be affected by retirements over the next decade;
- the information agencies have used and presently use to guide the identification of the probable effects of retirement and how agencies determine appropriate courses of action;
- strategies that have been taken or will be taken regarding recruiting, hiring, and retaining older workers; and
- characteristics and scope of these strategies, including human capital authorities or special legislation regarding flexibilities that are available to them.

To identify and describe alternative strategies, we performed a literature search and conducted interviews with government and private sector experts. The strategies that we describe were developed by the Departments of Agriculture, HUD, and State, the Internal Revenue Service (IRS), Environmental Protection Agency (EPA), and Nuclear Regulatory Commission (NRC). We selected these strategies because they were developed internally to met specific agency needs but could be used elsewhere in the government.

Observations On How Strategies Position Federal Agencies to Engage and Retain Older Workers

To address this objective, we reviewed previous GAO work and conducted interviews with federal officials at OPM and selected agencies and experts at AARP and other organizations that serve older individuals to determine how the federal government is progressing toward becoming a model employer. We chose the AARP criteria for selecting the best employers for workers over age 50 to compare to characteristics of federal employment because of its exclusive focus on older workers.

We conducted our work from November 2007 to April 2008 in accordance with generally accepted government auditing standards. Those standards require that we plan and perform the audit to obtain sufficient appropriate evidence to provide a reasonable basis for our findings and conclusions based on our audit objectives. We believe that the evidence obtained provides a reasonable basis for our findings and conclusions based on our audit objectives.

References

[1] See, for example, GAO, Highlights of a GAO Forum: Engaging and Retaining Older Workers, GAO-07-438SP (Washington, D.C.: February 2007); AARP, The Business Case for Workers Age 50+, (Washington, D.C.:2005); Partnership for Public Service, A Golden Opportunity: Recruiting Baby Boomers Into Government, (Washington, D.C.: January 2008); Department of Labor, Report of the Taskforce on the Aging of the American Workforce, (Washington, D.C.: February 2008).

[2] Pub.L. No. 101-576 (1990), as amended. The CFO Act agencies are 24 major executive agencies that are subject to the CFO Act. In 2007, the CFO Act agencies employed 98 percent of federal employees.

[3] For more information, see GAO, Redefining Retirement: Options for Older Americans, GAO-05-620T (Washington, D.C.: April 2005).

[4] GAO, Human Capital: Succession Planning and Management Is Critical Driver of Organizational Transformation, GAO-04-127T (Washington, D.C.: Oct. 1, 2003).

[5] These agencies were the Departments of Commerce, Education, Health and Human Services, Labor, Transportation, and the Treasury; the Equal Employment Opportunity Commission, Small Business Administration, and the Social Security Administration.

[6] Department of Labor, Report of the Taskforce on the Aging of the American Workforce, (Washington, D.C.: February 2008).

[7] We define retirement eligibility as being eligible for an unreduced (full) annuity. The specific rules vary by retirement plan. Under the Civil Service Retirement System (CSRS), the minimum age and service requirements are age 55 with 30 years of federal service, and under the Federal Employees Retirement System (FERS), the minimum age is between 55 and 57 (depending upon year of birth) and 30 years of service. In both CSRS and FERS, employees are also eligible to retire at either age 60 with 20 years of service, or age 62 with 5 years of service if they had federal careers shorter than 30 years by the time they were 60 or 62.

[8] According to OPM data, as of 2004, for voluntary retirements, retirement-eligible employees stay an average of 3.1 years before actually retiring.

[9] 9OPM, Human Resources in the Federal Government Flexibiities and Authorities, January 2008.

[10] See 5 C.F.R part 316, subpart D.

[11] This allows federal agencies to bring in temporary assignees for the mutual benefit of the federal government and the nonfederal entity. See 5 U.S.C. §§ 3371-3375, 5 C.F.R. part 334.

[12] See 5 C.F.R. part 300, subpart D.

[13] See 5 U.S.C. § 3109, 5 C.F.R. part 304.

[14] See 5 C.F.R. part 300, subpart E.

[15] See 5 U.S.C. § 8344 and § 8468, 5 C.F.R. part 553.

[16] Some agencies have agency-specific dual compensation waivers.

[17] This authority expires December 31, 2011.

[18] See 5 U.S.C. § 3304(a)(3), 5 C.F.R. part 337, subpart B.

[19] See 5 C.F.R. part 307.

[20] See 5 U.S.C. § 6303(e) and 5 C.F.R. 630.205.
[21] AARP, Staying Ahead of the Curve: The AARP Working and Retirement Study. (Washington, D.C.: September 2003)
[22] See 5 U.S.C. § 3402, 5 C.F.R. part 340, subparts A and B.
[23] See 5 U.S.C. § 6122, 5 C.F.R. part 610, subpart D.
[24] See, e.g., § 359 of Pub. L. No 106-346 (October 2000).
[25] See 5 U.S.C. §§ 5753-5754, 5 C.F.R. part 575, subparts A, B, and C.
[26] See 5 U.S.C. § 5377 and OPM Bulletin No. 9 1-09.
[27] See 5 U.S.C. § 5948, 5 C.F.R. part 595.
[28] See 5 U.S.C. § 5371.
[29] We used data from SSA's 2008 Retirement Wave Report. We did not independently verify reliability. Data used by SSA are generally consistent with data used by OPM.
[30] While using waiver authorities to rehire annuitants, SSA had also received a waiver to offer early retirement to some employees. Agency officials told us that the purpose of this waiver was to "right size" or free up resources to hire workers in positions where they are most needed.
[31] According to State Department officials, the Department has received some dual compensation waivers for specific Civil Service positions, such as those located in Iraq or for work in support of processing passports. These waivers allow Civil Service retirees to return to work earning full salaries and full annuity payments. The Department of State can hire back Foreign Service retirees on an intermittent schedule with full salaries and annuities up to certain limits if the Secretary authorizes.
[32] Pub. L. No. 98-313.
[33] NRCS developed ACES under the authority of section 1242(b)(4) of Title II of the Farm Security and Rural Investment Act of 2002.
[34] Partnership for Public Service, A Golden Opportunity: Recruiting Baby Boomers Into Government, (Washington, D.C.: January 2008). We found the methodology used by the Partnership to be sufficiently reliable for our use, including the survey methodology used to determine how many older workers think applying for a federal job is difficult.
[35] General Services Administration Modernization Act, Pub. L. No. 109-313 (Oct. 6, 2006).
[36] See S.2003 and HR.3579 relating to dual compensation waiver authority and HR.2780 relating to part time work for retirement annuity computation.
[37] AARP, formerly named the American Association of Retired Persons, is now known as AARP.

In: Federal Workforce Trends
Editor: Claude R. Lewis
ISBN 978-1-60692-830-1

Chapter 3

HUMAN CAPITAL: TRANSFORMING FEDERAL RECRUITING AND HIRING EFFORTS*

Robert N. Goldenkoff

WHY GAO DID THIS STUDY

To address the challenges that the nation faces, it will be important for federal agencies to change their cultures and create the institutional capacity to become high-performing organizations. This includes recruiting and retaining a federal workforce able to create, sustain, and thrive in organizations that are flatter, results-oriented, and externally focused.

In 2001, GAO identified strategic human capital management as a governmentwide high-risk area because federal agencies lacked a strategic approach to human capital management that integrated human capital efforts with their missions and program goals. Although progress has been made since that time, strategic human capital management still remains a high-risk area.

This testimony, based on a large body of completed work issued from January 2001 through April 2008, focuses on (1) challenges that federal agencies have faced in recruiting and hiring talented employees, (2) progress in addressing these challenges, and (3) additional actions that are needed to strengthen recruiting and

* This is and edited, excerpted and augmented edition of an United States Government Accountability Office publication GAO-08-762T, dated May 8, 2008.

hiring efforts. In its prior reports, GAO has made a range of recommendations to the Office of Personnel Management (OPM)— the government's personnel agency—and to agencies in such areas as hiring, workforce planning, and diversity management; a number of these recommendations have since been implemented. GAO is making no new recommendations at this time.

WHAT GAO FOUND

Numerous studies over the years have identified a range of problems and challenges with recruitment and hiring in the federal government. Some of these problems and challenges include passive recruitment strategies, unclear job vacancy announcements, and manual processes that are time consuming and paperwork intensive. In recent years, Congress, OPM, and agencies have made important strides in improving federal recruitment and hiring. For example, Congress has provided agencies with hiring flexibilities that could help to streamline the hiring process. OPM has sponsored job fairs and developed automated tools. Individual agencies have developed targeted recruitment strategies to identify and help build a talented workforce.

Building on the progress that has been made, additional efforts are needed in the following areas.

Human capital planning: Federal agencies will have to bolster their efforts in strategic human capital planning to ensure that they are prepared to meet their current and emerging hiring needs. Agencies must determine the critical skills and competencies necessary to achieve programmatic goals and develop strategies that are tailored to address any identified gaps.

Diversity management: Developing and maintaining workforces that reflect all segments of society and our nation's diversity is another significant aspect of agencies' recruitment challenges. Recruitment is a key first step toward establishing a diverse workforce. Agencies must consider active recruitment strategies, such as building formal relationships with targeted schools and colleges, and partnering with multicultural professional organizations.

Use of existing flexibiities: Agencies need to reexamine the flexibilities provided to them under current authorities, including monetary recruitment and retention incentives, special hiring authorities, and work-life programs. Agencies can then identify those existing flexibilities that could be used more extensively or more effectively to meet their workforce needs.

OPM leadership: OPM has taken significant steps in fostering and guiding improvements in recruiting and hiring in the executive branch. For example,

OPM, working with and through the Chief Human Capital Officers Council, has moved forward in compiling information on effective and innovative practices and sharing this information with agencies. Still, OPM must continue to work to ensure that agencies take action on this information. Also, OPM needs to make certain that it has the internal capacity to guide agencies' readiness to implement change and achieve desired outcomes.

OPM and agencies should be held accountable for the ongoing monitoring and refinement of human capital approaches to recruit and hire a capable and committed federal workforce. With continued commitment and strong leadership, the federal government can indeed be an employer of choice.

Mr. Chairman and Members of the Subcommittee:

Thank you for the opportunity to be here today to discuss recruiting and hiring of the next generation of federal employees. Today's hearing coincides with Public Service Recognition Week, which honors the men and women who serve America as federal, state, and local government employees. We commend the subcommittee for this opportunity to highlight the progress that the federal government has made in improving its recruitment and hiring practices over the past few years as well as draw attention to the continued challenges and opportunities facing federal agencies in acquiring capable and committed employees.

The importance of a top-notch federal workforce cannot be overstated. The nation is facing new and more complex challenges in the 21st century as various forces are reshaping the United States and its place in the world. These forces include a large and growing long-term fiscal imbalance, evolving national and homeland security threats, increasing global interdependence, and a changing economy. Further, as we have pointed out in our High-Risk Series and other reports for Congress, some federal agencies continue to face persistent performance and accountability problems at a time when taxpayers have come to expect— and need—higher levels of performance and greater responsiveness by public officials and programs.

To address these challenges, it will be important for federal agencies to change their cultures and create the institutional capacity to become high-performing organizations. This includes recruiting and retaining employees able to create, sustain, and thrive in organizations that are flatter, results-oriented, and externally focused and that collaborate with other governmental entities as well as with the private and nonprofit sectors to achieve desired outcomes.

As you are aware, in 2001, we identified federal human capital management as a governmentwide high-risk area because federal agencies lacked a strategic approach to human capital management that integrated human capital efforts with their missions and program goals.[1] Although progress has been made since that time, strategic human capital management still remains on our high-risk list.[2] As we have previously reported in our work on human capital issues, federal agencies do not consistently have the modern human capital programs and policies needed to ensure that they have the right people in the right jobs at the right time to meet the challenges they face.[3]

Exacerbating this problem, governmentwide, about one-third of federal employees on board at the end of fiscal year 2007 will become eligible to retire by 2012. Proportions of workers eligible to retire are projected to be especially high in certain occupations—some of them mission critical—as well as in key leadership positions. Indeed, as we recently reported, about 51 percent of customs and border protection agents, 58 percent of air traffic controllers, 85 percent of administrative law judges, and 64 percent of career executives may be eligible to retire by 2012.[4]

That said, the way forward is not gloomy. In many ways, the federal government is well positioned to acquire, develop, and retain the people it needs to carry out its diverse roles and responsibilities. Importantly, federal employment offers rewards, such as interesting work and opportunities to make a difference in the lives of others, as well as a variety of tangible benefits and work-life flexibilities that make an organization an employer of choice.[5] Moreover, the Office of Personnel Management (OPM) and agencies have made noteworthy progress in addressing the various human capital challenges they face, often in response to our findings and recommendations. For example:

- OPM identified additional human capital flexibilities and worked to build consensus for legislative change;
- the Office of Management and Budget directed agencies to adopt a strategic approach to acquisition workforce planning; and
- the Department of Housing and Urban Development prepared a strategic workforce plan to be better prepared to recruit and hire the people it needs to fulfill its mission.

As requested, my testimony today will focus on (1) challenges that federal agencies have faced in recruiting and hiring talented employees, (2) the progress that has been made to date in addressing these challenges, and (3) additional actions that are needed moving forward to strengthen the government's recruiting and hiring efforts. My remarks today will underscore the following: Improving the federal recruiting and hiring process to attract the next generation of federal employees is a shared responsibility between the federal government's central personnel agency—OPM, individual agencies, and Congress. With sustained and committed leadership, innovation, and planning, the federal government can brand itself as an employer of choice and successfully compete in the labor market for its fair share of the nation's best and brightest individuals.

This testimony is based on a large body of our completed work issued from January 2001 through April 2008. Our previous work included reviews of OPM and agency documents related to federal hiring, studies on recruiting and hiring that were completed by other organizations in recent years, as well as data from OPM's central database of governmentwide personnel information. We also interviewed various officials from OPM, the interagency Chief Human Capital Officers Council, and selected federal agencies. We performed our performance audits in accordance with generally accepted government auditing standards. Those standards require that we plan and perform the audit to obtain sufficient, appropriate evidence to provide a reasonable basis for our findings and conclusions based on our audit objectives. We believe that the evidence obtained provides a reasonable basis for our findings and conclusions based on our audit objectives.

FEDERAL RECRUITING AND HIRING HAS BEEN A LONG-STANDING CHALLENGE

For years it has been widely recognized that the federal hiring process all too often does not meet the needs of (1) agencies in achieving their missions; (2) managers in filling positions with the right talent; and (3) applicants for a timely, efficient, transparent, and merit-based process. In short, the federal hiring process is often an impediment to the very customers it is designed to serve in that it makes it difficult for agencies and managers to obtain the right people with the right skills, and applicants can be dissuaded from public service because of the complex and lengthy procedures.

Numerous studies over the past decade by OPM, the Merit Systems Protection Board (MSPB), the National Academy of Public Administration, the Partnership for Public Service, the National Commission on the Public Service, and GAO have identified a range of problems and challenges with recruitment and hiring in the federal government, including the following:[6]

- Passive recruitment strategies.
- Poor and insufficient workforce planning.
- Unclear job vacancy announcements.
- Time-consuming and paperwork-intensive manual processes.
- Imprecise candidate assessment tools.
- Ineffective use of existing hiring flexibilities.

These problems put the federal government at a serious competitive disadvantage in acquiring talent. For example, passive recruitment strategies, such as infrequent or no outreach to college campuses, miss opportunities to expose potential employees to information about federal jobs. Unclear and unfriendly vacancy announcements can cause confusion for applicants, delay hiring, and serve as poor recruiting tools. Weak candidate assessment tools can inadequately predict future job performance and result in the hiring of individuals who do not fully possess the appropriate skills for the job. As evidence of these and other problems, MSPB's most recently published Merit Principles Survey results found that only 5 percent of federal managers and supervisors said that they faced no significant barriers to hiring employees for their agencies.[7]

Congress, OPM, and Agencies have Taken Significant Steps to Help Improve Recruiting and Hiring

In recent years, Congress, OPM, and agencies have taken a series of important actions to improve recruiting and hiring in the federal sector. For example, Congress has provided agencies with hiring flexibilities that could help agencies streamline their hiring processes and give agency managers more latitude in selecting among qualified job candidates. Congress has also provided several agencies with exemptions from the pay and classification restrictions of the General Schedule. Other examples of congressional action related to recruitment and hiring follow.

Dual compensation waivers to rehire federal retirees. OPM may grant waivers allowing agencies to fill positions with rehired federal annuitants without offsetting the salaries by the amount of the annuities.[8] Agencies can request waivers on a case-by-case basis for positions that are extremely difficult to fill or for emergencies or other unusual circumstances. Agencies can also request from

OPM a delegation of authority to grant waivers for emergencies or other unusual circumstances.

- Special authority to hire for positions in contracting. Agencies can rehire federal annuitants to fill positions in contracting without being required to offset the salaries. Agencies are required only to notify and submit their hiring plans to OPM.[9]
- Enhanced annual leave computation. Agencies may credit relevant private sector experience when computing annual leave amounts.[10]

As the federal government's central personnel management agency, OPM has a key role in helping agencies acquire, develop, retain, and manage their human capital. In the areas of recruiting and hiring, OPM has, for example, done the following.

- Sponsored job fairs across the country and produced television commercials to make the public more aware of the work that federal employees do.
- Developed a 45-day hiring model to help agencies identify the steps in their processes that tend to bog them down, and created a detailed checklist to assist agencies in undertaking a full-scale makeover of their hiring process from beginning to end.
- Developed a Hiring Tool Kit on its Web site that is to aid agencies in improving and refining their hiring processes and that includes a tool to assist agency officials in determining the appropriate hiring flexibilities to use given their specific situations.
- Updated and expanded its report Human Resources Flexibilities and Authorities in the Federal Government, which serves as a handbook for agencies in identifying current flexibilities and authorities and how they can be used to address human capital challenges.
- Established standardized vacancy announcement templates for common occupations, such as secretarial, accounting, and accounting technician positions, into which agencies can insert summary information concerning their specific jobs prior to posting for public announcement.

Individual federal agencies have also taken actions to meet their specific recruitment and hiring needs. For example:

- The National Aeronautics and Space Administration (NASA) has used a combination of techniques to recruit workers with critical skills, including targeted recruitment activities, educational outreach programs, improved compensation and benefits packages, professional development programs, and streamlined hiring authorities.[11] Many of NASA's external hires have been for entry-level positions through the Cooperative Education Program, which provides NASA centers with the opportunity to develop and train future employees and assess the abilities of potential employees before making them permanent job offers.
- The Nuclear Regulatory Commission (NRC) has endeavored to align its human capital planning framework with its strategic goals and has identified the activities needed to achieve a diverse, skilled workforce and an infrastructure that supports the agency's mission and goals.[12] NRC has used various flexibilities in recruiting and hiring new employees, and it has tracked the frequency and cost associated with the use of some flexibilities. While there was room for further improvement, NRC has been effective in recruiting, developing, and retaining a critically skilled workforce.

Additional Actions are Needed to Strengthen Recruiting and Hiring

While these actions are all steps in the right direction, our past work has found that additional efforts are needed in the areas of strategic human capital planning, diversity management, and the use of existing flexibilities. In addressing these areas, agency managers need to be held accountable for maximizing the efficiency and effectiveness of their recruiting efforts and hiring processes. In addition, OPM, working with and through the Chief Human Capital Officers Council, must use its leadership position to vigorously and convincingly encourage continuous improvement in agencies and provide appropriate assistance to support agencies' recruitment and hiring efforts. In carrying out its important role, OPM will need to ensure that it has the internal capacity to assist and guide agencies' readiness to implement needed improvements. I will discuss each one of these areas in turn.

Human Capital Planning

First and foremost, federal agencies will have to bolster their efforts in strategic human capital planning to ensure that they are prepared to meet their current and emerging hiring needs. To build effective recruiting and hiring programs, agencies must determine the critical skills and competencies necessary to achieve programmatic goals and develop strategies that are tailored to address any identified gaps. For example, an agency's strategic human capital plan should address the demographic trends that the agency faces with its workforce, especially pending retirements. We have found that leading organizations go beyond a succession planning approach that focuses on simply replacing individuals; instead, agencies should consider their future mission requirements and the knowledge, skills, and abilities needed to meet those requirements.[13]

Recruiting and hiring for the acquisition workforce is a prime example of the government's strategic human capital planning challenges. Acquisition of products and services from contractors consumes about a quarter of discretionary spending governmentwide and is a key function in many federal agencies. We have reported that many acquisition professionals need to acquire a new set of skills focusing on business management because of a more sophisticated business environment.[14] At a GAO-sponsored forum in July 2006, acquisition experts reported that agency leaders had not recognized or elevated the importance of the acquisition profession within their organizations, and a strategic approach had not been taken across government or within agencies to focus on workforce challenges, such as creating a positive image essential to successfully recruiting and retaining a new generation of talented acquisition professionals.[15]

Diversity Management

Developing and maintaining workforces that reflect all segments of society and our nation's diversity is another significant aspect of agencies' recruitment challenges. As we have previously reported, recruitment is a key first step toward establishing a diverse workforce.[16] To ensure that they are reaching out to diverse pools of talent, agencies must consider active recruitment strategies, such as the following:

- Widening the selection of schools from which they recruit to include, for example, historically Black colleges and universities, Hispanic- serving institutions, women's colleges, and schools with international programs.

- Building formal relationships with targeted schools and colleges to ensure the cultivation of talent for future applicant pools.
- Partnering with multicultural professional organizations and speaking at their conferences to communicate their commitment to diversity to external audiences and strengthen and maintain relationships.

For these types of recruitment strategies, agencies can calculate the cost of recruiting channels and cross-reference those costs with the volume and quality of candidates yielded in order to reallocate funds to the most effective recruiting channels.

Several agencies have taken steps toward developing and implementing active recruitment strategies that take into account a diverse pool of job candidates. For example:

- NASA developed a strategy for recruiting Hispanics that focuses on increasing educational attainment, beginning in kindergarten and continuing into college and graduate school, with the goal of attracting students into the NASA workforce and aerospace community. NASA said it must compete with the private sector for the pool of Hispanics qualified for aerospace engineering positions, which is often attracted by more-lucrative employment opportunities in the private sector in more preferable locations.[17] NASA centers sponsored, and its employees participated in, mentoring, tutoring, and other programs to encourage Hispanic and other students to pursue careers in science, engineering, technology, and mathematics.
- An official with the National Institute of Standards and Technology (NIST) said that when NIST hosted recruitment or other programs, it made use of relationships the agency had with colleges, universities, and other groups to inform students about internship or employment opportunities.[18] One group that helped to arrange such recruitment efforts was the National Organization of Black Chemists and Black Chemical Engineers. The NIST official said that NIST had been active in the professional organization's leadership for years and that NIST employees had served on its executive board. Another NIST official said that the professional organization had helped with NIST's efforts to recruit summer interns.
- The Federal Aviation Administration (FAA) developed internship opportunities designed to recruit a diverse group of future candidates for the agency.[19] Its Minority-Serving Institutions Internship Program was

designed to provide professional knowledge and experience at FAA or firms in the private sector for minority students and students with disabilities who are enrolled in a college or university, major in relevant fields and related disciplines, and have a minimum of a 3.0 grade point average. Students in the internship program could earn academic credit for their participation during the fall or spring semesters or over the summer.

Use of Existing Flexibilities

Additionally, the appropriate use of human capital flexibilities is crucial to making further improvements in agencies' efforts to recruit, hire, and manage their workforces. Federal agencies often have varied statutory authorities related to workforce management.[20] These authorities provide agencies with flexibility in helping them manage their human capital strategically to achieve results. In previous reports and testimonies, we have emphasized that in addressing their human capital challenges, federal agencies should first identify and use the flexibilities already available under existing laws and regulations and then seek additional flexibilities only when necessary and based on sound business cases. Our work has found that the insufficient and ineffective use of these existing flexibilities can significantly hinder the ability of federal agencies to recruit, hire, retain, and manage their human capital.[21]

The ineffective use of available hiring flexibilities represents a lost opportunity for agencies to effectively manage human capital. In 2002, Congress provided agencies with two new hiring flexibilities.[22] One of these hiring flexibilities, known as category rating, permits an agency to select best-qualified job candidates for a position rather than being limited to the three top-ranked job candidates. The other hiring flexibility, often referred to as direct hire, allows an agency to appoint people to positions without adherence to certain competitive examination requirements when there is a severe shortage of qualified candidates or a critical hiring need. However, we have found that agencies were making limited use of these available flexibilities.[23] Various agency officials from across the federal government often had previously cited both of these hiring flexibilities as needed tools to help in improving the federal hiring process.

Agencies need to reexamine the flexibilities provided to them under current authorities and identify those that could be used more extensively or more effectively to meet their workforce needs. Our prior work hasn identified several human capital flexibilities that agency officials and union representatives frequently cited as most effective for managing their workforces.[24] These flexibilities encompass broad areas of personnel- related actions that could be especially beneficial for agencies' recruiting and hiring efforts. They include monetary recruitment and retention incentives; special hiring authorities, such as student employment programs; and work-life programs, such as alternative work schedules, child care assistance, and transit subsidies.

OPM Leadership

As part of its key leadership role, OPM has taken significant steps in fostering and guiding improvements in recruiting and hiring in the executive branch. Still, OPM must continue to assist—and as appropriate, require—the building of the infrastructures within agencies needed to successfully implement and sustain human capital reforms to strengthen recruitment and hiring. OPM can do this in part by encouraging continuous improvement and providing appropriate assistance to support agencies' recruitment and hiring efforts. Innovative and best practices of model agencies need to be made available to other agencies in order to facilitate the transformation of agency hiring practices from compliance based to agency mission based. OPM, working with and through the Chief Human Capital Officers Council, has made progress in compiling information on effective and innovative practices and distributing this information to help agencies in determining when, where, and how the various flexibilities are being used and should be used. OPM must continue to work to ensure that agencies take action on this information.

Moreover, in leading governmentwide human capital reform, OPM has faced challenges in its internal capacity to assist and guide agencies' readiness to implement change. In October 2007, we issued a report on the extent to which OPM has (1) addressed key internal human capital management issues identified through employee survey responses and (2) put in place strategies to ensure that it has the mission-critical talent it needs to meet current and future strategic goals.[25] We found that OPM has taken positive actions to address specific concerns raised by its employees and managers in the employee surveys. We also found that OPM has strategies in place, such as workforce and succession management plans, that are aligned with selected leading practices relevant to the agency's capacity to fulfill its strategic goals. However, OPM lacks a well-documented agencywide evaluation process of some of its workforce planning efforts. In a relatively short time, there will also be a presidential transition, and well-documented processes can help to ensure a seamless transition that builds on the current momentum.

Equally important is OPM's leadership in federal workforce diversity and oversight of merit system principles. In our review of how OPM and the Equal Employment Opportunity Commission (EEOC) carry out their mutually shared responsibilities for helping to ensure a fair, inclusive, and nondiscriminatory federal workplace, we found limited coordination between the two agencies in policy and oversight matters.[26] The lack of a strategic partnership between the two agencies and an insufficient understanding of their mutual roles, authority, and responsibilities can result in a lost opportunity to realize consistency, efficiency, and public value in federal equal employment opportunity and workplace diversity human capital management practices. We recommended that OPM and EEOC regularly coordinate in carrying out their responsibilities under the equal employment opportunity policy framework and seek opportunities for streamlining like reporting requirements. Both agencies acknowledged that their collaborative efforts could be strengthened but took exception to the recommendation to streamline requirements. We continue to believe in the value of more collaboration.

Finally, OPM and agency leaders need to be held accountable and should hold others accountable for the ongoing monitoring and refinement of human capital approaches to recruit and hire a capable and committed federal workforce. Leadership is critical for agencies to overcome their natural resistance to change, to marshal the resources needed in many cases to improve management, to build and maintain organizationwide commitment to improving their ways of doing business, and to create the conditions for effectively improving human capital approaches. Some agency officials have told us that OPM rules and regulations are rigid, yet agency officials are also often hesitant to implement new approaches without specific guidance. It will be important for agencies and OPM to define their appropriate roles and day-to-day working relationships as they collaborate on developing and implementing innovative and more effective recruitment efforts and hiring processes.

In conclusion, OPM and agencies have made progress in addressing the impediments to effective recruitment and hiring since we first designated strategic human capital management as a high-risk area in 2001. Still, as I have discussed today, more can be done. Faced with a workforce that is becoming more retirement eligible and finding gaps in talent because of changes in the knowledge, skills, and competencies in occupations needed to meet their missions, agencies must strengthen their recruiting and hiring efforts. Moreover, human capital expertise within the agencies must be up to the challenge for this transformation to be successful and enduring. With an ongoing commitment to continuous improvement and strong leadership in Congress, OPM, and the agencies, the federal government can indeed be an employer of choice.

REFERENCES

[1] GAO, High-Risk Series: An Update, GAO-01-263 (Washington, D.C.: January 2001).
[2] GAO, High-Risk Series: An Update, GAO-07-310 (Washington, D.C.: January 2007).
[3] GAO, Human Capital: Federal Workforce Challenges in the 21st Century, GAO-07-556T (Washington, D.C.: Mar. 6, 2007).
[4] GAO, Older Workers: Federal Agencies Face Challenges, but Have Opportunities to Hire and Retain Experienced Employees, GAO-08-630T (Washington, D.C.: Apr. 30, 2008).
[5] As reported in the Merit Systems Protection Board's Merit Principles Survey 2005, which obtained federal employees' views on how well the workforce is being managed
[6] See, for example, GAO, Human Capital: Opportunities to Improve Executive Agencies' Hiring Processes, GAO-03-450 (Washington, D.C.: May 30, 2003); Human Capital: Additional Collaboration Between OPM and Agencies Is Key to Improved Federal Hiring, GAO-04-797 (Washington, D.C.: June 7, 2004); and Human Capital: Status of Efforts to Improve Federal Hiring, GAO-04-796T (Washington, D.C.: June 7, 2004). Also, see Merit Systems Protection Board, Reforming Federal Hiring: Beyond Faster and Cheaper (Washington, D.C.: September 2006).
[7] Merit Systems Protection Board, Accomplishing Our Mission: Results of the Merit Principles Survey 2005 (Washington, D.C.: February 2007).
[8] See 5 U.S.C. § 8344 and § 8468, 5 C.F.R. part 553.
[9] This authority expires December 31, 2011.
[10] See 5 U.S.C. § 6303(e) and 5 C.F.R. 630.205.
[11] GAO, NASA: Progress Made on Strategic Human Capital Management, but Future Program Challenges Remain, GAO-07-1004 (Washington, D.C.: Aug. 8, 2007).
[12] GAO, Human Capital: Retirements and Anticipated New Reactor Applications Will Challenge NRC's Workforce, GAO-07-105 (Washington, D.C.: Jan. 17, 2007).

[13] GAO, Human Capital: Succession Planning and Management Is Critical Driver of Organizational Transformation, GAO-04-127T (Washington, D.C.: Oct. 1, 2003).
[14] GAO, Acquisition Workforce: Status of Agency Efforts to Address Future Needs,
[15] GAO-03-55 (Washington, D.C.: Jan. 17, 2003).
[16] GAO, Highlights of a GAO Forum: Federal Acquisition Challenges and Opportunities in the 21st Century, GAO-07-45SP (Washington, D.C.: Oct. 6, 2006).
[17] GAO, Diversity Management: Expert-Identified Leading Practices and Agency Examples, GAO-05-90 (Washington, D.C.: Jan. 14, 2005).
[18] GAO, The Federal Workforce: Additional Insights Could Enhance Agency Efforts Related to Hispanic Representation, GAO-06-832 (Washington, D.C.: Aug. 17, 2006).
[19] GAO-05-90.19GAO-05-90
[20] GAO, Human Capital: Selected Agencies' Statutory Authorities Could Offer Options in Developing a Framework for Governmentwide Reform, GAO-05-398R (Washington, D.C.: Apr. 21, 2005).
[21] GAO, Human Capital: Effective Use of Flexibilities Can Assist Agencies in Managing Their Workforces, GAO-03-2 (Washington, D.C.: Dec. 6, 2002).
[22] These hiring flexibilities are contained in the Chief Human Capital Officers Act of 2002, Title XIII of the Homeland Security Act of 2002. Pub. L. No. 107-296 (Nov. 25, 2002).
[23] GAO, Human Capital: Increasing Agencies' Use of New Hiring Flexibilities, GAO-04-959T (Washington, D.C.: July 13, 2004)
[24] GAO-03-2.
[25] GAO, Office of Personnel Management: Opportunities Exist to Build on Recent Progress in Internal Human Capital Capacity, GAO-08-11 (Washington, D.C.: Oct. 31, 2007)..
[26] GAO, Equal Employment Opportunity: Improved Coordination Needed between EEOC and OPM in Leading Federal Workplace EEO, GAO-06-214 (Washington, D.C.: June 16, 2006).

INDEX

D

E

R

S